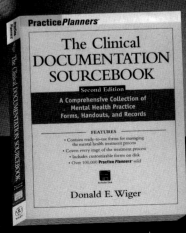

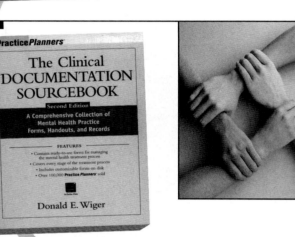

YEA OR NAY?

Many decisions are made by comparing the advantages and disadvantages of each possible alternative. It can be helpful to spell these out so you can compare your options. This form is designed to help you do that.

1. State two options open to you.
   1. _____
   2. _____

2. State alternative action 1 and list its pros and cons.

   Action to be taken: _____

   Pros   *Cons*

   _____   _____

   _____   _____

   _____   _____

   _____   _____

   _____   _____

3. For each of the disadvantages (cons), list your ideas for how you could deal with it so it is no longer a problem.

   _____

   _____

   _____

   _____

   _____

4. What role does this decision play in your life's work?

   _____

   _____

   _____

5. How would a decision for or against help you fulfill your purpose in life?

   _____

   _____

   _____

6. State alternative action 2 and list its pros and cons.

   Action to be taken: _____

   Pros   *Cons*

   _____   _____

   _____   _____

   _____   _____

   _____   _____

   _____   _____

7. For each of the disadvantages (cons), list your ideas for how you could deal with it so it is no longer a problem.

   _____

   _____

   _____

   _____

   _____

8. What role does this decision play in your life's work?

   _____

   _____

   _____

9. How would a decision for or against help you fulfill your purpose in life?

   _____

   _____

   _____

Remember to bring completed work sheet to your next appointment

Practice*Planners*™

Treatment Planners cover all the necessary elements for developing formal treatment plans, including detailed problem definitions, long-term goals, short-term objectives, therapeutic interventions, and DSM-IV diagnoses.

❏ **The Complete Adult Psychotherapy Treatment Planner, Second Edition**
277pp / 0-471-31924-4 / $39.95

❏ **The Child and Adolescent Psychotherapy Treatment Planner**
240pp / 0-471-15647-7 / $39.95

❏ **The Chemical Dependence Treatment Planner**
256pp / 0-471-23795-7 / $39.95

❏ **The Continuum of Care Treatment Planner**
170pp / 0-471-19568-5 / $39.95

❏ **The Couples Therapy Treatment Planner**
272pp / 0-471-24711-1 / $39.95

❏ **The Employee Assistance (EAP) Treatment Planner**
176pp / 0-471-24709-X / $39.95

❏ **The Pastoral Counseling Treatment Planner**
176pp / 0-471-25416-9 / $39.95

❏ **The Older Adult Psychotherapy Treatment Planner**
274pp / 0-471-29574-4 / $39.95

❏ **The Behavioral Medicine Treatment Planner**
226pp / 0-471-31923-6 / $39.95

Homework Planners feature dozens of behaviorally-based, ready-to-use assignments which are designed for use between sessions... as well as a disk (Microsoft Word) containing all of the assignments, allowing you customize them to suit your unique style and your clients' needs.

❏ **Brief Therapy Homework Planner**
236pp / 0-471-24611-5 / $49.95

❏ **Brief Couples Therapy Homework Planner**
208pp / 0-471-29511-6 / $49.95

❏ **Brief Child Therapy Homework Planner**
304pp / 0-471-32366-7 / $49.95

❏ **Brief Adolescent Therapy Homework Planner**
304pp / 0-471-34465-6 / $49.95

Documentation Sourcebooks provide all the forms and records that therapists need to meet the documentation requirements of the managed care era. All of the documents are also provided on disk so they can be easily customized.

❏ **The Clinical Documentation Sourcebook, Second Edition**
304pp / 0-471-32692-5 / $49.95

❏ **The Psychotherapy Documentation Primer**
203pp / 0-471-28990-6 / $39.95

❏ **The Couple & Family Clinical Documentation Sourcebook**
176pp / 0-471-25234-4 / $49.95

❏ **The Child Clinical Documentation Sourcebook**
256pp / 0-471-29111-0 / $49.95

❏ **The Chemical Dependence Treatment Documentation Sourcebook**
320pp / 0-471-31285-1 / $49.95

❏ **The Forensic Documentation Sourcebook**
224pp / 0-471-25459-2 / $75.00

Name _____

Affiliation _____

Address _____

City/State/Zip _____

Phone/Fax _____

Email _____

To order, call 800-225-5945
(Please refer to promo #063 0-4052 A when ordering.)

or, send this page, with payment, to:
John Wiley & Sons, Inc, Attn: M. Fellin,
605 Third Ave., New York, NY 10157-0228

❏ Check enclosed   ❏ Visa   ❏ Mastercard   ❏ American Express

Card # _____

Expiration Date _____

Signature _____

* Please add your local sales tax to all orders.

www.wiley.com/practiceplanners

Brief Therapy
Homework Planner

PRACTICE PLANNER SERIES PREFACE

The practice of psychotherapy has a dimension that did not exist 30, 20, or even 15 years ago—accountability. Treatment programs, public agencies, clinics, and even group and solo practitioners must now justify the treatment of patients to outside review entities that control the payment of fees. This development has resulted in an explosion of paperwork.

Clinicians must now document what has been done in treatment, what is planned for the future, and what the anticipated outcomes of the interventions are. The books and software in this Practice Planner series are designed to help practitioners fulfill these documentation requirements efficiently and professionally.

The Practice Planner series is growing rapidly. It now includes not only the original *Complete Psychotherapy Treatment Planner* and the *Child and Adolescent Psychotherapy Treatment Planner*, but also *Treatment Planners* targeted to speciality areas of practice, including: chemical dependency, the continuum of care, couples therapy, group therapy, employee assistance, pastoral counseling, and more.

In addition to the *Treatment Planners*, the series also includes *TheraScribe®: The Computerized Assistant to Psychotherapy Treatment Planning* and other software designed to streamline office management, as well as adjunctive books, such as the *Brief Therapy Homework Planner* and *Clinical Documentation Planner*, aimed at aiding in practice management. The goal of the series is to provide practitioners with the resources they need in order to provide high-quality care in the era of accountability—or, to put it simply, we seek to help you spend more time on patients, and less on paperwork.

ARTHUR E. JONGSMA, JR.
Grand Rapids, Michigan

Brief Therapy
Homework Planner

Gary M. Schultheis

John Wiley & Sons, Inc.
New York • Chichester • Weinheim • Brisbane • Singapore • Toronto

---

Note about Photocopy Rights

The publisher grants purchasers permission to reproduce handouts from this book for professional use with their clients.

Library of Congress Cataloging-in-Publication Data:
Schultheis, Gary M.
    Brief therapy homework planner / by Gary M. Schultheis.
       p.   cm.—(Psychotherapy treatment planners)
    Includes bibliographical references.
    ISBN 0-471-24611-5 (pbk./disk : alk. paper)
    1. Brief psychotherapy—Problems, exercises, etc. 2. Solution-
focused therapy—Problems, exercises, etc. I. Title. II. Series.
RC480.55.S38   1998
616.89'14—dc21   97-41088
                                                              CIP

Printed in the United States of America

10 9 8 7 6

PREFACE

WHY HOMEWORK?

Although many therapists can remember the days when they were discouraged from suggesting that a client take any particular action, "homework" assignments—exercises assigned to a client to complete between sessions—have now become an accepted adjunct to the therapeutic process. Extracurricular assignments allow the clients to take what they have discussed in therapy, and try it in the "real world." In my own practice, I've found that homework can be a valuable means of:

- Introducing change.
- Encouraging experimentation.
- Engaging the client in therapy.
- Evoking resources.
- Highlighting something that happened in the session.
- Focusing attention on an issue.
- Searching for solutions.

HOW TO USE THIS BOOK

Most of the assignments used in this book are based on the solution-oriented approach to therapy. With minor adaptations, the exercises should be applicable regardless of your preferred mode of therapy. The book is designed so that you can quickly photocopy an exercise and hand the assignment to your client.

Alternatively, you can use these exercises as springboards for your own custom-tailored homework assignments. To adapt the exercises, just slip the word-processing disk into your computer, and make a copy of the exercise you have chosen. You can then fine-tune the material to make the assignment your own. You might paste your letterhead at the top of the page. Use your client's name. Work your client's language and metaphors into the assignment. Delete questions you don't like. Rewrite the introductory paragraph.

Break the rules. Invite your client to help you. Don't forget to have fun, at least some of the time. And make sure you follow up—these exercises are not meant for self-help use; they are designed to be used and processed with the help of a therapist.

ORGANIZATION OF THE EXERCISES

The 62 exercises in this book are clustered into 18 sections on the basis of the skills, feelings, or ideas the client is working on. Although the exercise titles suggest what the assignment seeks to address, skim through the *Brief Therapy Homework Planner* and familiarize yourself with each assignment. Then, as the client focuses on specific skills or issues that would benefit from between-sessions work, you can quickly select an appropriate homework assignment.

The exercises are also cross-listed by some of the behavioral problems for which the exercise is most appropriate (e.g., anxiety, dependency, vocational stress, etc.). Although these cross-references may help you identify the right exercise for the right situation, don't feel locked in by the specific behavioral problem. Remember, you can and should customize the assignments to fit the client's needs and your therapeutic style.

CARRYING OUT THE ASSIGNMENTS

There are three stages of therapy homework: (1) assigning the homework, (2) completing the homework, and (3) follow-up on the homework.

In assigning homework, I frequently frame it as an experiment. This approach has several advantages. One is that it conveys the unspoken message that I (the therapist) don't have the answers. Framing the exercise as experimentation implies a value of flexibility that clients often take and run with. When the client performs an exercise, things either improve or they don't. Either way, important information is gathered that can inform the next action to be taken by both the therapist and the client.

Sometimes clients ask why I have designed an assignment in a particular way. I answer them as honestly as possible, even if the answer is, "Just to do something different and see what happens." Whenever possible, I like to encourage a playful attitude. I prefer for the client to be involved in the development of the exercise and to feel free to make alterations as he or she sees fit. I often explain to clients that when I make suggestions or ask questions, my primary purpose is usually not to provide information for me. Instead, it is because I think that in answering a question or performing an action, a client is likely to do something that will lead to a solution. I frequently suggest that clients feel free to alter or discontinue the assignment on their own. I want the client to be at least as active in the assignment as I am.

Once the client has completed the assignment, it is important to explore the answers he or she arrived at. What results did the experiment yield? To help get things started, each assignment contains some suggestions for areas you may want to explore in the session(s) after the client completes the exercise.

I hope this book provides a springboard for your own creativity.

GARY SCHULTHEIS
Evansville, Indiana

ACKNOWLEDGMENTS

I want to thank a few folks who helped me with this project. First, thanks to Bill O'Hanlon for what he has taught me over the past nine years and for suggesting me for this project. I'm very grateful to Kelly Franklin, senior editor at John Wiley & Sons, who conceived this book and guided me through the entire process. Thanks to Alexandra Mummery at Wiley for a lot of formatting and fine-tuning. Richard Rust, Fred Walborn, Hanns Pieper, and the members of MFTC-L listserv have influenced and challenged me with their ideas in countless conversations. Finally, a big thank-you to my wife, Sandy, who has helped me with my homework for the past 19 years.

CONTENTS

Section I

SET GOALS

FROM HERE TO WHERE?

GOALS OF THE EXERCISE

1. To encourage the client to clarify what he or she wants.
2. To suggest that the client focus on the client's own behavior rather than the actions of others.

TYPES OF PROBLEMS THIS EXERCISE MAY BE MOST USEFUL FOR

- Adjustment disorder.
- Anger management.
- Anxiety.
- Chemical dependence/relapse.
- Childhood trauma.
- Dependency.
- Depression.
- Dissociation.
- Eating disorder.
- Family conflict.
- Female sexual dysfunction.
- Grief/loss unresolved.
- Impulse control disorder.
- Intimate relationship conflict.
- Low self-esteem.
- Male sexual dysfunction.
- Mania or hypomania.
- Obsessive-compulsive behavior.
- Paranoid ideation.
- Phobia-panic/agoraphobia.
- Psychoticism.
- Sexual abuse.
- Sleep disturbance.

- Social discomfort.
- Somatization.
- Spiritual confusion.
- Suicidal ideation.
- Type A behavior.
- Vocational stress.

SUGGESTIONS FOR PROCESSING THIS EXERCISE WITH CLIENT

a. How will you know therapy has been successful?
b. What will be or what has been the first small sign of change?
c. What will you do to encourage change to continue?

FROM HERE TO WHERE?

The great philosopher and Yankee catcher Yogi Berra said, "You have got to be very careful if you don't know where you are going, because you might not get there." Do you know where you want to go? This exercise may help you decide. Take as much time as you need to complete it.

1. Between now and your next session, make a list of the things you would like to change. Be specific. Cite particular events or experiences. Focus on what you do or experience in the situation, rather than how you want others to change.

_____

_____

_____

_____

2. When you are finished with counseling, what will be different? What could change to make you say to yourself, "Getting into counseling and doing the work I did there was one of the best things I've ever done"?

_____

_____

_____

3. What will be (or has been) the first and smallest sign that change is beginning?

_____

_____

_____

4. When you notice that first change, what can you do to keep the ball rolling?

_____

_____

_____

Remember to bring completed work sheet to your next appointment

SO WHAT?

GOALS OF THE EXERCISE

1. To suggest that the client connect problems to larger themes in his or her life.
2. To invite the client to think about the relevance of the problem in the client's life.
3. To explore the client's ideas about the necessity of taking action.

TYPES OF PROBLEMS THIS EXERCISE MAY BE MOST USEFUL FOR

- Adjustment disorder.
- Anger management.
- Antisocial behavior.
- Anxiety.
- Chemical dependence/relapse.
- Dependency.
- Depression.
- Eating disorder.
- Educational deficit.
- Family conflict.
- Impulse control disorder.
- Intimate relationship conflict.
- Low self-esteem.
- Obsessive-compulsive behavior.
- Phobia-panic/agoraphobia.
- Spiritual confusion.

SUGGESTIONS FOR PROCESSING THIS EXERCISE WITH CLIENT

a. What do you want to change?
b. Why is this important?
c. How does this issue relate to the important things in your life?
d. How does success in this situation affect the way you think about yourself?

SO WHAT?

Sometimes we set long-term goals, but forget that everyday activities influence one's ability to achieve these goals. It can be helpful to make the connection.

1. State what you want to change.

   _____

   _____

2. In what ways is what you want to change currently a problem for you?

   _____

   _____

   _____

3. How does what you want to change influence what others think of you?

   _____

   _____

   _____

4. How does what you want to change impact what you think of yourself?

   _____

   _____

   _____

5. How does what you want to change affect your ability to do the work that gives your life meaning?

   _____

   _____

   _____

6. What will happen if you don't make any changes?

   _____

   _____

   _____

7. What does it say about you that you would make the kinds of changes you are planning?

_____

_____

_____

Remember to bring completed work sheet to your next appointment

Section II

WATCH WHAT YOU SAY

DEFINING THE PROBLEM

GOALS OF THE EXERCISE

1. To suggest to the client that the way the client sees the problem may be important.
2. To help the client identify alternative ways of conceiving of the problem.
3. To encourage the client to reframe the problem as something the client does or controls, rather than as something that is done to the client.

TYPES OF PROBLEMS THIS EXERCISE MAY BE MOST USEFUL FOR

- Adjustment disorder.
- Anger management.
- Antisocial behavior.
- Anxiety.
- Chemical dependence/relapse.
- Childhood trauma.
- Dependency.
- Depression.
- Dissociation.
- Eating disorder.
- Educational deficit.
- Family conflict.
- Female sexual dysfunction.
- Grief/loss unresolved.
- Impulse control disorder.
- Intimate relationship conflict.
- Legal conflict.
- Low self-esteem.
- Male sexual dysfunction.
- Mania or hypomania.
- Obsessive-compulsive behavior.

- Paranoid ideation.
- Phobia-panic/agoraphobia.
- Psychoticism.
- Sexual abuse.
- Sleep disturbance.
- Social discomfort.
- Somatization.
- Spiritual confusion.
- Suicidal ideation.
- Type A behavior.
- Vocational stress.

SUGGESTIONS FOR PROCESSING THIS EXERCISE WITH CLIENT

a. What actions or events are at the heart of the problem?
b. When and how does the problem manifest itself behaviorally?
c. What are the consequences of the problem?
d. What do you control?

DEFINING THE PROBLEM

> The ways in which we think about our world have a major impact on our actions and feelings. Some ways of thinking make it more likely that you will find a way to solve the problem you are having. This exercise is designed to help you conceive of the difficulties you are having in new ways. Try it with each problem you want to work on.

1. Describe the problem.

   _____

   _____

   _____

2. Restate the problem in the past tense (e.g., "We never get along" could become "We've had trouble getting along lately").

   _____

   _____

   _____

3. What changed in your life or behavior prior to the last occurrence of the problem?

   _____

   _____

   _____

4. Describe the problem in terms of specific actions and incidents, and give three examples (e.g., the global problem "I am irresponsible" can be illustrated specifically as "I overdrew my checking account last week").

   1. _____
   2. _____
   3. _____

5. Characterize the problem in terms of how it affects your day-to-day life by listing three specific consequences of the problem (e.g., the consequences of losing your temper might be "My kids avoid me because they don't know when I'm going to explode" or "I have a hard time keeping a job because I tend to yell at my coworkers").

1. _____

2. _____

3. _____

6. Even if the problem involves other people, restate it in a way that allows you to take responsibility for your behavior in the problem situation (e.g., "My husband puts me down" can be restated as "I have tolerated my husband's abusive language for five years").

_____

_____

_____

7. Review your responses to the questions and restate your problem in a way that makes you feel most hopeful about finding a solution.

_____

_____

_____

Remember to bring completed work sheet to your next appointment

TRUTH IN LABELING

GOALS OF THE EXERCISE

1. To help the client start thinking about self differently.
2. To encourage the client to stop placing negative labels on self.
3. To suggest that the client can learn new ways of seeing self.

TYPES OF PROBLEMS THIS EXERCISE MAY BE MOST USEFUL FOR

- Anger management.
- Anxiety.
- Chemical dependence/relapse.
- Dependency.
- Depression.
- Family conflict.
- Intimate relationship conflict.
- Low self-esteem.
- Obsessive-compulsive behavior.
- Phobia-panic/agoraphobia.
- Social discomfort.
- Type A behavior.

SUGGESTIONS FOR PROCESSING THIS EXERCISE WITH CLIENT

a. How have you thought about yourself in the past?
b. Has the way you have thought about yourself in the past helped you?
c. Are your labels accurate?
d. What would be a more accurate way of thinking about yourself?
e. If a client insists on keeping a negative label, explore the possibility that the label does not tell the whole truth and that there may also be some positive ways of characterizing oneself.

TRUTH IN LABELING

Most of us know that words can have a strong impact on us, but we remain unaware of how negative labels and characterizations close off the possibility (in our own minds) that we or others can act differently. This is an exercise in becoming aware of the labels you use and in identifying some alternatives to this labeling.

1. Write 10 words (more would be better) that you use to describe yourself.

   1. _____   6. _____
   2. _____   7. _____
   3. _____   8. _____
   4. _____   9. _____
   5. _____   10. _____

2. Place a check mark by the words you consider to be negative.

3. Do the negative labels help you in dealing with the problem? If so, how?

   _____
   _____
   _____

4. For each negative label or characterization, list at least three experiences in your life when you proved the inaccuracy of the label (e.g., "I'm just a lazy slug" could be countered by "Last Saturday I finally washed that sinkful of dishes I had saved up for two weeks").

   _____
   _____
   _____
   _____
   _____
   _____
   _____
   _____
   _____
   _____

5. If a label is entirely accurate, there can be no exceptions. If the label is not accurate, it might be better to discontinue using it. For each negative label or characterization, write a sentence about yourself that more accurately describes your behavior.

    _____

    _____

    _____

Suggestion: When you find that you are verbally degrading yourself, ease up and make sure that you are being accurate in your characterization of yourself.

Remember to bring completed work sheet to your next appointment

GET A (NEW) JOB

GOALS OF THE EXERCISE

1. To help the client reframe the situation.
2. To suggest that the client can do something worthwhile even while experiencing a situation that is less than ideal.
3. To add some humor to the situation.
4. To help the client bring meaning to an unpleasant experience.

TYPES OF PROBLEMS THIS EXERCISE MAY BE MOST USEFUL FOR

- Anger management.
- Family conflicts (parent-child).
- Vocational stress.

SUGGESTIONS FOR PROCESSING THIS EXERCISE WITH CLIENT

a. What do you already know about running and ruining a business?
b. How can you put this knowledge to good use?

Note: I have used this exercise in situations where my clients needed to remain in a job until they found another. It could easily be changed for other situations (e.g., a teen writing about parenting until able to move out of the house). The idea was inspired by Jay Haley's essays "How to Have an Awful Marriage" and "How to Be a Failure as a Therapist" in *The Power Tactics of Jesus Christ and Other Essays.*

GET A (NEW) JOB

Give yourself a new job. You can continue working for your current employer, but your new job is as a freelance writer doing research for an article that describes how to run a business poorly. Be aware that it is necessary do certain things in order to make a business fail, and it is your job to research every one of them. Each mistake your employer makes should help you with your article.

Answering the following questions may give you some ideas.

1. Describe the managerial attitude that guarantees failure in business.

   _____

   _____

   _____

2. List five actions that contribute to failure that you have already learned from your employer.

   1. _____
   2. _____
   3. _____
   4. _____
   5. _____

3. What actions cause employees to feel as if they have failed?

   _____

   _____

   _____

4. What are some of the things that your employer has done in the past that could have accidentally caused success?

   _____

   _____

   _____

5. List three publications that may be interested in your article.

   1. _____

   2. _____

   3. _____

6. How can you use this experience to help you do the work that gives your life meaning?

_____

_____

_____

Remember to bring completed work sheet to your next appointment

Section III

IDENTIFY EXCEPTIONS TO THE PROBLEM

TRACK THE PROBLEM/SOLUTIONS

GOALS OF THE EXERCISE

1. To invite the client to look at the problem in more detail and with an eye toward finding solutions.
2. To further suggest that the client may be able to affect the problem.

TYPES OF PROBLEMS THIS EXERCISE MAY BE MOST USEFUL FOR

- Adjustment disorder.
- Anger management.
- Antisocial behavior.
- Anxiety.
- Chemical dependence/relapse.
- Childhood trauma.
- Dependency.
- Depression.
- Dissociation.
- Eating disorder.
- Family conflict.
- Female sexual dysfunction.
- Grief/loss unresolved.
- Impulse control disorder.
- Intimate relationship conflict.
- Legal conflict.
- Low self-esteem.
- Male sexual dysfunction.
- Mania or hypomania.
- Medical issue.
- Obsessive-compulsive behavior.
- Paranoid ideation.
- Phobia-panic/agoraphobia.

- Psychoticism.
- Sexual abuse.
- Sleep disturbance.
- Social discomfort.
- Somatization.
- Spiritual confusion.
- Suicidal ideation.
- Type A behavior.
- Vocational stress.

SUGGESTIONS FOR PROCESSING THIS EXERCISE WITH CLIENT

a. When was the problem less serious?
b. What did you do to influence the severity of the problem?
c. What did you learn from this exercise?

TRACK THE PROBLEM/SOLUTIONS

At the end of each day, take the time to review the severity of the problem over the course of that day. Create an imaginary and personal scale ranging from zero to 10 to show the magnitude of the problem. Zero can represent the problem not existing and 10 can represent the problem being worse than it ever has been. Give your experience of the problem an overall number rating for the day, or take two numbers that describe the high and low points of the day and average them, or record both. Chart your daily number(s) on the graph. Note the things you did during each day that made the problem better or at least not worse than it was.

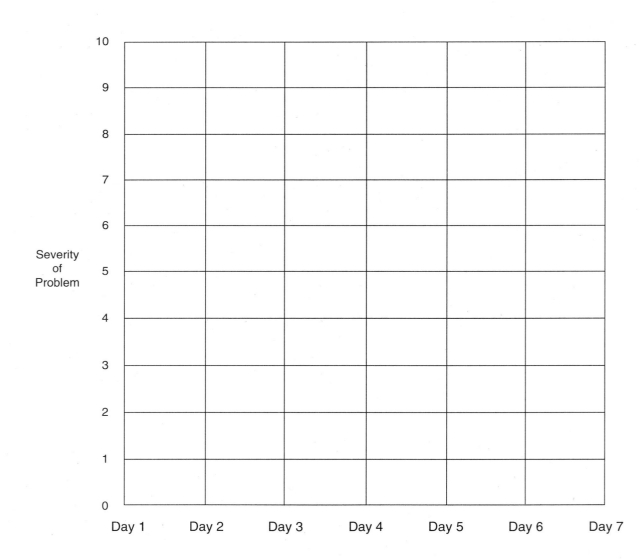

Severity of Problem

10
9
8
7
6
5
4
3
2
1
0

Day 1   Day 2   Day 3   Day 4   Day 5   Day 6   Day 7

Day 1

_____

_____

_____

Day 2

_____

_____

_____

Day 3

_____

_____

_____

Day 4

_____

_____

_____

Day 5

_____

_____

_____

Day 6

_____

_____

_____

Day 7

_____

_____

_____

Remember to bring completed work sheet to your next appointment

EVERYDAY EXCEPTIONS

GOALS OF THE EXERCISE

1. To suggest that there are exceptions to the problem.
2. To help the client identify things she or he already does that help to solve the problem.

TYPES OF PROBLEMS THIS EXERCISE MAY BE MOST USEFUL FOR

- Adjustment disorder.
- Anger management.
- Antisocial behavior.
- Anxiety.
- Chemical dependence/relapse.
- Childhood trauma.
- Dependency.
- Depression.
- Dissociation.
- Eating disorder.
- Family conflict.
- Female sexual dysfunction.
- Grief/loss unresolved.
- Impulse control disorder.
- Intimate relationship conflict.
- Low self-esteem.
- Mania or hypomania.
- Obsessive-compulsive behavior.
- Phobia-panic/agoraphobia.
- Sexual abuse.
- Social discomfort.
- Somatization.
- Spiritual confusion.

- Suicidal ideation.
- Type A behavior.
- Vocational stress.

SUGGESTIONS FOR PROCESSING THIS EXERCISE WITH CLIENT

a. How can you explain why sometimes the problem is better or gone entirely?
b. What does it say about you that you sometimes do things that affect the severity of the problem?
c. Based on what you have learned, what will you do now?

EVERYDAY EXCEPTIONS

Each day note three things that you do *not* want to change in regard to the problem situation. Take note of the times when you feel better or when you notice that the problem is not as much of a problem as it usually is. What is it that you do to make each of these things happen or continue to happen?

Day 1

    1. _____

    2. _____

    3. _____

Day 2

    1. _____

    2. _____

    3. _____

Day 3

    1. _____

    2. _____

    3. _____

Day 4

    1. _____

    2. _____

    3. _____

Day 5

    1. _____

    2. _____

    3. _____

Day 6

    1. _____

    2. _____

    3. _____

Day 7

1. _____

2. _____

3. _____

Remember to bring completed work sheet to your next appointment

ASK FOR HELP

GOALS OF THE EXERCISE

1. To normalize the problem situation.
2. To encourage the client to seek out and use resources already available.
3. To help the client build a support network.

TYPES OF PROBLEMS THIS EXERCISE MAY BE MOST USEFUL FOR

- Adjustment disorder.
- Anger management.
- Anxiety.
- Chemical dependence/relapse.
- Childhood trauma.
- Cognitive deficit.
- Dependency.
- Depression.
- Eating disorder.
- Educational deficit.
- Family conflict.
- Grief/loss unresolved.
- Intimate relationship conflict.
- Low self-esteem.
- Medical issue.
- Obsessive-compulsive behavior.
- Phobia-panic/agoraphobia.
- Psychoticism.
- Sexual abuse.
- Sleep disturbance.
- Social discomfort.
- Spiritual confusion.
- Suicidal ideation.

- Type A behavior.
- Vocational stress.

SUGGESTIONS FOR PROCESSING THIS EXERCISE WITH CLIENT

a. How did you decide on whom you would ask for help?
b. How did you ask for help and what did you say?
c. How will you use the advice you received?

ASK FOR HELP

> Many of us feel that we must solve our own problems independently, as if that were really possible, and we therefore don't think to ask for help.

1. List five or more people you know have had or think have had a problem similar to yours at one time or another. Feel free to include in your list one or two persons from history or from the world of fiction.

   1. _____
      _____

   2. _____
      _____

   3. _____
      _____

   4. _____
      _____

   5. _____
      _____

2. Go to at least three of these people and, after explaining your situation, ask them for their advice or assistance. Pay close attention to any skills they mention that they use to help fix their problems. Record their responses after their names.

3. What surprised you about their responses?

   _____
   _____
   _____
   _____

4. How has this exercise influenced your thinking about the problem and how you can solve it?

   _____
   _____
   _____
   _____

5. How will this influence your behavior?

_____

_____

_____

_____

_____

Remember to bring completed work sheet to your next appointment

CATCH 'EM IN THE ACT

GOALS OF THE EXERCISE

1. To suggest that the client's own actions may influence the behavior of others.
2. To help the client anticipate situations and to plan a response.
3. To encourage the client to try something different if one type of action doesn't work.
4. To suggest that the client focus on what he or she really wants.

TYPES OF PROBLEMS THIS EXERCISE MAY BE MOST USEFUL FOR

- Anger management.
- Antisocial behavior.
- Dependency.
- Depression.
- Family conflicts.
- Intimate relationship conflicts.
- Low self-esteem.

SUGGESTIONS FOR PROCESSING THIS EXERCISE WITH CLIENT

a. What do you want to change?
b. How can you communicate your desires to others?
c. What happened when you tried to make your wishes known?

CATCH 'EM IN THE ACT

It is usually easy for most of us to identify things that we don't like or that cause us pain. While this a very valuable survival skill, we often take for granted the things we *do* like. Spotlighting the positive can have a dramatic effect on behavior, especially in situations that involve others.

1. Make a list of actions, relevant to the problem you are working on, that you would like the other person(s) to do more often. Be as specific and clear as possible. You may want to think in terms of small steps in the right direction. Add to your list between now and your next session.

   _____   _____
   _____   _____
   _____   _____
   _____   _____
   _____   _____

2. For each of the actions listed above, devise three responses that will let the other person(s) know that you like what they are doing. Be specific about what words you will use and about what actions you will take. Remember that communication can take many forms.

   _____
   _____
   _____
   _____
   _____
   _____
   _____
   _____
   _____
   _____

3. Try your ideas and record the responses to your new behavior.

   _____
   _____

_____

_____

_____

_____

_____

_____

_____

_____

4. If you were not satisfied with the responses you received from the other person(s), what did you try next to let them know you appreciated their original behavior?

_____

_____

_____

_____

_____

_____

_____

Remember to bring completed work sheet to your next appointment

Section IV

PLOT A STRATEGY

MAP THE PROBLEM

GOALS OF THE EXERCISE

1. To help the client reframe the problem as a series of steps.
2. To suggest that the client's behavior affects the problem sequence, and whether it is maintained or changed.

TYPES OF PROBLEMS THIS EXERCISE MAY BE MOST USEFUL FOR

- Adjustment disorder.
- Anger management.
- Antisocial behavior.
- Anxiety.
- Chemical dependence/relapse.
- Childhood trauma.
- Dependency.
- Depression.
- Dissociation.
- Eating disorder.
- Family conflict.
- Female sexual dysfunction.
- Impulse control disorder.
- Intimate relationship conflict.
- Legal conflict.
- Low self-esteem.
- Male sexual dysfunction.
- Mania or hypomania.
- Obsessive-compulsive behavior.
- Paranoid ideation.
- Phobia-panic/agoraphobia.
- Psychoticism.
- Sleep disturbance.

- Social discomfort.
- Somatization.
- Spiritual confusion.
- Suicidal ideation.
- Type A behavior.
- Vocational stress.

SUGGESTIONS FOR PROCESSING THIS EXERCISE WITH CLIENT

a. If you wanted to make the problem happen, what would you do to make that more likely?
b. What tells you the problem is starting?
c. Does anything you do keep the problem going? If so, how? (What is your part of the dance that keeps the problem going?)
d. Explore the step-by-step description of the problem and see how the client might do something to get a different result.

MAP THE PROBLEM

This is an exercise in observation, both of yourself and of others who might be involved in the problem situation. Between now and your next session, observe yourself and others when the problem arises. Spell out specifically what typically happens when the problem occurs. The more details you include, the more helpful this exercise is likely to be. Take notes as the problem unfolds if you need to. If more than one person is involved in the problem, it may be helpful for each person to do this exercise.

1. When does the problem usually happen?

   _____

   _____

   _____

2. When does the problem rarely happen?

   _____

   _____

   _____

3. Where does the problem usually happen?

   _____

   _____

   _____

4. Where does the problem rarely happen?

   _____

   _____

   _____

5. Are there any other constants you can identify regarding when the problem happens and when it doesn't (e.g., clothing or things you tell yourself)?

   _____

   _____

   _____

6. What is your first inkling that the problem is starting? Be specific about words, body language, actions, and voicing.

   _____

   _____

   _____

7. How do you respond? Be specific about words, body language, actions, and voicing.

   _____

   _____

   _____

8. How does the other person respond to the same situation? Be specific about words, body language, actions, and voicing.

   _____

   _____

   _____

9. Write a detailed step-by-step account or draw a flowchart of how the problem typically unfolds. Use the back of the page or another sheet of paper if necessary.

   _____

   _____

   _____

   _____

   _____

   _____

   _____

   _____

   _____

Remember to bring completed work sheet to your next appointment

GET OUTTA HERE!

GOALS OF THE EXERCISE

1. To suggest that the client can think of the problem as being outside oneself.
2. To imply that the client can do something about the problem.
3. To invite the client to recall past successes.
4. To encourage the client to review the way the client thinks about himself or herself.

TYPES OF PROBLEMS THIS EXERCISE MAY BE MOST USEFUL FOR

- Anger management.
- Anxiety.
- Chemical dependence/relapse.
- Childhood trauma.
- Depression.
- Eating disorder.
- Family conflict.
- Impulse control disorder.
- Low self-esteem.
- Obsessive-compulsive behavior.
- Paranoid ideation.
- Phobia-panic/agoraphobia.
- Social discomfort.
- Suicidal ideation.
- Type A behavior.
- Vocational stress.

SUGGESTIONS FOR PROCESSING THIS EXERCISE WITH CLIENT

a. Describe the problem.
b. How does the problem influence you?
c. What are some things you might want to do more frequently?
d. What do your successes say about you?

GET OUTTA HERE!

It can be easy to start to think you are the problem, especially if you and others keep saying you are. Keep in mind that you are not the problem. Here are some suggestions to help you remember that.

1. Give the problem a name (e.g., Stinky, Count Depressula, or ♥, "the performer formerly known as Mother").

   _____

2. What are eight words you would use to describe your problem to a friend?

   1. _____   5. _____

   2. _____   6. _____

   3. _____   7. _____

   4. _____   8. _____

3. Is this problem male, female, neuter, or other?

   _____

4. What does he/she/it look like? Describe the problem with words or a picture.

   _____

   _____

   _____

5. How has the problem tricked you into doing something that wasn't in your best interest?

   _____

   _____

   _____

   _____

6. What does the problem tell you about yourself?

   _____

   _____

   _____

7. When and how do you stand up to the problem?

_____

_____

_____

_____

8. What does it say about you that you sometimes stand up to the problem?

_____

_____

_____

_____

Suggestion: Try thinking of the problem by the name you have given it and see if you can catch the problem trying to trick or entice you into acting as if you are the problem. Have a conversation with the problem and set him/her/it straight.

Remember to bring completed work sheet to your next appointment

MAKE A DEADLINE

GOALS OF THE EXERCISE

1. To encourage the client to set a deadline that has consequences if the client does not follow through.
2. To frame goal accomplishment as a series of steps.

TYPES OF PROBLEMS THIS EXERCISE MAY BE MOST USEFUL FOR

- Adjustment disorder.
- Anger management.
- Antisocial behavior.
- Anxiety.
- Chemical dependence/relapse.
- Childhood trauma.
- Cognitive deficit.
- Dependency.
- Depression.
- Dissociation.
- Eating disorder.
- Educational deficit.
- Family conflict.
- Female sexual dysfunction.
- Grief/loss unresolved.
- Impulse control disorder.
- Intimate relationship conflict.
- Legal conflict.
- Low self-esteem.
- Male sexual dysfunction.
- Mania or hypomania.
- Obsessive-compulsive behavior.
- Paranoid ideation.

- Phobia-panic/agoraphobia.
- Psychoticism.
- Sexual abuse.
- Sleep disturbance.
- Social discomfort.
- Somatization.
- Spiritual confusion.
- Suicidal ideation.
- Type A behavior.
- Vocational stress.

SUGGESTIONS FOR PROCESSING THIS EXERCISE WITH CLIENT

a. Did you meet your deadline?
b. If not, do you think you need to make your steps smaller or to give yourself a consequence that will have more of an impact? What other alternatives are there?
c. If the client didn't follow through, you may want to discuss motivation.

MAKE A DEADLINE

Sometimes natural consequences are not sufficient motivating factors. At those times it can be helpful to remember that you can motivate yourself. This exercise offers some suggestions for doing that.

1. State the thing you want to accomplish in clear terms.

    _____

    _____

    _____

2. Set a final deadline for your project.

    _____

3. Divide this project into at least 10 distinct smaller steps, each with its own deadline.

    1. _____   6. _____

    2. _____   7. _____

    3. _____   8. _____

    4. _____   9. _____

    5. _____   10. _____

4. For the odd-numbered steps, set a reward for accomplishing the task on time.

    1. _____

    3. _____

    5. _____

    7. _____

    9. _____

5. For the even-numbered steps, set a negative consequence for not accomplishing the task on time.

    2. _____

    4. _____

    6. _____

    8. _____

    10. _____

Try to follow through with your plan and then answer the following questions:

6. How did you convince yourself to accomplish each step?

_____

_____

_____

_____

7. Were you more motivated by the rewards or by the negative consequences?

_____

_____

_____

Remember to bring completed work sheet to your next appointment

WRITE YOUR OWN SCRIPT

GOALS OF THE EXERCISE

1. To encourage the client to take time to think about all the roles the client plays in life.
2. To suggest that the client has some choice in the roles chosen and in how they are played.
3. To remind the client that change may bring difficulties that then can be dealt with.
4. To propose that life has a purpose that is reflected in daily activities.

TYPES OF PROBLEMS THIS EXERCISE MAY BE MOST USEFUL FOR

- Adjustment disorder.
- Anxiety.
- Chemical dependence/relapse.
- Dependency.
- Depression.
- Family conflict.
- Intimate relationship conflict.
- Low self-esteem.
- Obsessive-compulsive behavior.

SUGGESTIONS FOR PROCESSING THIS EXERCISE WITH CLIENT

a. What roles do you play in your life?
b. How would you like to change the descriptions of the roles you play?
c. What might make it difficult for you to change?
d. How do your everyday activities fit into the big picture of your life?

WRITE YOUR OWN SCRIPT

> We all fill a number of roles in our lives. These roles are defined both by others and by ourselves. We often grow into and accept these role definitions without thinking about them consciously. This exercise invites you to examine and revise some of the roles you play.

1. List six of the roles you play in your life. Think of the relationships you have and what is expected of you in those relationships (e.g., father, housekeeper, community member).

   1. _____   4. _____

   2. _____   5. _____

   3. _____   6. _____

2. Write a "job description" for each role. Make a list that states specifically every task or responsibility that goes with that role as you now fill it or as you feel is expected of you. Use separate pages for this part of the exercise.

3. Rewrite each job description so that is it reasonable and so that it balances the welfare of yourself with the welfare of others. Remember to define where each responsibility should end. If duties are duplicated in different roles, include the duplicated duty in each job description.

4. How would others react if you were to start using the rewritten job descriptions to guide your actions? Be specific about how each individual would react.

   _____

   _____

   _____

   _____

   _____

   _____

5. What difficulties can you anticipate in your "new job" and what steps can you take to prevent or deal with them?

   _____

   _____

_____
_____
_____
_____

6. How does each role relate to the work that gives your life meaning?

_____
_____
_____
_____
_____
_____

7. Are there any roles you would like to give up?

_____
_____
_____
_____
_____
_____

Remember to bring completed work sheet to your next appointment

THERE'S USUALLY MORE THAN ONE WAY . . .

GOALS OF THE EXERCISE

1. To suggest a split between values and the ways in which they get expressed.
2. To challenge the client to be flexible and creative in one's thinking.

TYPES OF PROBLEMS THIS EXERCISE MAY BE MOST USEFUL FOR

- Anger management.
- Anxiety.
- Dependency.
- Depression.
- Family conflict.
- Intimate relationship conflict.
- Legal conflict.
- Obsessive-compulsive behavior.
- Sleep disturbance.
- Type A behavior.
- Vocational stress.

SUGGESTIONS FOR PROCESSING THIS EXERCISE WITH CLIENT

a. What values are important to you?
b. How have you tried to solve the problem?
c. What ideas did you come up with when you were brainstorming?
d. Which of these ideas do you want to try?

THERE'S USUALLY MORE THAN ONE WAY . . .

It's easy to get stuck by thinking in repetitive patterns. Sometimes it's helpful to distinguish between what you want to accomplish and the actions you take to go about doing that. Remember that there may be more than one way to get from here to there. This exercise encourages you to use your imagination to generate some new ideas.

1. Think about the thing you want to change. Write it here:

   _____

   _____

   _____

2. What values are at stake (i.e., why is this important to you?)?

   _____

   _____

   _____

3. What efforts have you made so far?

   _____

   _____

   _____

4. Looking at the values you have, brainstorm 10 other ways to achieve your goals (in brainstorming, the goal is to use your imagination and come up with as many ideas as possible with little or no regard for their practicality).

   1. _____   6. _____
   2. _____   7. _____
   3. _____   8. _____
   4. _____   9. _____
   5. _____   10. _____

5. Put the paper away for three days.

6. Get the paper out again and come up with five more ideas.

    11. _____   14. _____

    12. _____   15. _____

    13. _____

7. Study your ideas and be prepared to discuss them along with whatever new ideas might be suggested in your next session.

    Remember to bring completed work sheet to your next appointment

EXPRESS IT DIFFERENTLY

WRITE IT

GOALS OF THE EXERCISE

1. To increase rapport with the client by joining him or her in attempts to solve the problem.
2. To give the client another way to express himself or herself.
3. To suggest that the client can learn from the experience.

TYPES OF PROBLEMS THIS EXERCISE MAY BE MOST USEFUL FOR

- Anxiety.
- Depression.
- Obsessive-compulsive behavior.
- Phobia-panic/agoraphobia.
- Sleep disturbance.

SUGGESTIONS FOR PROCESSING THIS EXERCISE WITH CLIENT

a. What did you learn about your problem from this exercise?
b. What did you learn about yourself from this exercise?
c. What do you need to do next?

I got this idea from Steve deShazer's book, *Keys to Solution in Brief Therapy*, and my clients have used it successfully many times.

WRITE IT

Decide on a 30-minute time period each day to work on your problem. If it is possible, try to do this exercise at the same time each day.

Find a quiet place and do what you can to ensure that you will have no distractions. Get out a pen and paper.

Set a timer for 30 minutes.

Put your problem down on paper. Write out whatever comes to mind. Keep the pen moving and don't censor what you write. If it's the same thing over and over, that's all right.

When the timer goes off, stop writing. Imagine you found this piece of paper on the side of the road and have no idea who did the writing. Answer the same four questions after each daily writing session.

In the days to come, if you find yourself thinking about the problem, gently remind yourself that you will have a full half hour to think about your problem and that you have more pressing matters to work on at present. If you think you might forget something that has occurred to you, you can make a note so you won't forget to think about it later. You should then return to your activity. If you find your problem returns, just remind yourself, gently, that you have more important things to do and that you will take care of the problem later.

At the end of each writing session, decide what you will do with the paper you have written. Do you want to destroy it now? How? Do you want to keep it? If so, how long will you keep it and how will you use it?

Day 1

1. How do you react to what you have read?

   _____

   _____

   _____

2. What can you learn from the person who wrote it?

   _____

   _____

   _____

3. What does the writer need to do or learn?

_____

_____

_____

4. What did you do with the paper? Why?

_____

_____

_____

Day 2

1. How do you react to what you have read?

_____

_____

_____

2. What can you learn from the person who wrote it?

_____

_____

_____

3. What does the writer need to do or learn?

_____

_____

_____

4. What did you do with the paper? Why?

_____

_____

_____

Day 3

1. How do you react to what you have read?

_____

_____

_____

2. What can you learn from the person who wrote it?

_____

_____

_____

3. What does the writer need to do or learn?

_____

_____

_____

4. What did you do with the paper? Why?

_____

_____

_____

Day 4

1. How do you react to what you have read?

_____

_____

_____

2. What can you learn from the person who wrote it?

_____

_____

_____

3. What does the writer need to do or learn?

_____

_____

_____

4. What did you do with the paper? Why?

_____

_____

_____

Day 5

1. How do you react to what you have read ?

_____

_____

_____

2. What can you learn from the person who wrote it?

_____

_____

_____

3. What does the writer need to do or learn?

_____

_____

_____

5. What did you do with the paper? Why?

_____

_____

_____

Day 6

1. How do you react to what you have read?

_____

_____

_____

2. What can you learn from the person who wrote it?

_____

_____

_____

3. What does the writer need to do or learn?

_____

_____

_____

4. What did you do with the paper? Why?

_____

_____

_____

Day 7

1. How do you react to what you have read?

_____

_____

_____

2. What can you learn from the person who wrote it?

_____

_____

_____

3. What does the writer need to do or learn?

_____

_____

_____

4. What did you do with the paper? Why?

_____

_____

_____

Remember to bring completed work sheet to your next appointment

MAKE A SYMBOL

GOALS OF THE EXERCISE

1. To suggest that problems can be addressed indirectly.
2. To encourage the client to do something different.
3. To imply that change will inevitably happen.
4. To invite the client to identify change when it happens.

TYPES OF PROBLEMS THIS EXERCISE MAY BE MOST USEFUL FOR

- Adjustment disorder.
- Anger management.
- Antisocial behavior.
- Anxiety.
- Chemical dependence/relapse.
- Childhood trauma.
- Cognitive deficit.
- Dependency.
- Depression.
- Dissociation.
- Eating disorder.
- Educational deficit.
- Family conflict.
- Female sexual dysfunction.
- Grief/loss unresolved.
- Impulse control disorder.
- Intimate relationship conflict.
- Legal conflict.
- Low self-esteem.
- Male sexual dysfunction.
- Mania or hypomania.
- Medical issue.

- Obsessive-compulsive behavior.
- Paranoid ideation.
- Phobia-panic/agoraphobia.
- Psychoticism.
- Sexual abuse.
- Sleep disturbance.
- Social discomfort.
- Somatization.
- Spiritual confusion.
- Suicidal ideation.
- Type A behavior.
- Vocational stress.

SUGGESTIONS FOR PROCESSING THIS EXERCISE WITH CLIENT

a. Please explain your symbol.
b. What have you learned about yourself?
c. How has your understanding of the problem changed?
d. What will you do with your symbol now? Why?

MAKE A SYMBOL

Symbols allow you to take a lot of information, put it into a neat package, and then manipulate it. When a judge wants the courtroom to quiet down, she raps her gavel and there is no need to explain who is in charge, where she gets her power, and what she wants. The symbol says it all. You can use the power of symbols in a variety of ways to help you manage problems that you face.

Within the next two days, find a symbol for your problem. Some places you might look could be:

A closet.   A hardware store.
Your garage.   A junkyard or junk store.
A toy store.   The woods or a forest.
An art supplies store.   The street.

If you are crafty, you might make it from:

Clay, FIMO®, or Sculpey®.
Wood.
Rock(s).
Yarn.
Food (could get messy, but don't rule out anything).

Carry your symbol with you for a month. Literally. Never let it be out of reach. Feel free to use your symbol in any way you think might be helpful in dealing with your problem. At the end of the month, answer the following questions. Wait until then to read them.

1. What have you learned about yourself during the past month?

   _____

   _____

   _____

2. What have you learned about the problem during the past month?

   _____

   _____

   _____

3. How has your relationship with the problem changed over the course of the past month?

_____

_____

_____

4. What do you want to do with your symbol now?

_____

_____

_____

5. How could it be helpful in the future?

_____

_____

_____

6. If you want to let go of it, what is the best way for you to do that? If you do, what will you be giving up?

_____

_____

_____

7. If you keep it, what will you do with it?

_____

_____

_____

Remember to bring completed work sheet to your next appointment

PICTURE THIS

GOALS OF THE EXERCISE

1. To encourage the client to look at the problem in a new way.
2. To suggest that the problem may be approached indirectly.
3. To provide a different way to express the problem.
4. To propose that the problem may have weaknesses that can be utilized.

TYPES OF PROBLEMS THIS EXERCISE MAY BE MOST USEFUL FOR

- Adjustment disorder.
- Anger management.
- Antisocial behavior.
- Anxiety.
- Chemical dependence/relapse.
- Childhood trauma.
- Dependency.
- Depression.
- Dissociation.
- Eating disorder.
- Educational deficit.
- Family conflict.
- Female sexual dysfunction.
- Grief/loss unresolved.
- Impulse control disorder.
- Intimate relationship conflict.
- Low self-esteem.
- Male sexual dysfunction.
- Mania or hypomania.
- Medical issue.
- Obsessive-compulsive behavior.
- Paranoid ideation.

- Phobia-panic/agoraphobia.
- Sexual abuse.
- Sleep disturbance.
- Social discomfort.
- Somatization.
- Spiritual confusion.
- Suicidal ideation.
- Type A behavior.
- Vocational stress.

SUGGESTIONS FOR PROCESSING THIS EXERCISE WITH CLIENT

a. Tell me about your picture.
b. What suggestions does this give you for actions you could take in the future?

PICTURE THIS

In the space below, make a picture of the problem.

Now put the picture away for a few days and then answer the questions on the next page.

Remember that there are no wrong answers. If you can't answer a question, you might want to try later.

Look at the picture again as if you have never seen it before and study it.

1. What do you notice now that you were not aware of before?

   _____

   _____

   _____

2. Musicians know the silence between the notes is at least as important as the notes themselves. Zen artists say the brush carries open space. Study the space in your picture. What does it suggest to you?

   _____

   _____

   _____

3. What weaknesses or vulnerabilities does the picture of the problem suggest to you?

   _____

   _____

   _____

4. Now you can add yourself to the picture, dealing with the problem successfully.

5. How might you use this image to help yourself in the future?

   _____

   _____

   _____

Remember to bring completed work sheet to your next appointment

UNFINISHED BUSINESS LETTER

GOALS OF THE EXERCISE

1. To suggest a safe way to express feelings.
2. To acknowledge the client's right to feelings.

TYPES OF PROBLEMS THIS EXERCISE MAY BE MOST USEFUL FOR

- Adjustment disorder.
- Grief/loss unresolved.
- Sexual abuse.

SUGGESTIONS FOR PROCESSING THIS EXERCISE WITH CLIENT

a. Allow the client to discuss the contents of the letter to the extent that is helpful.
b. What do you want to do with the letter?
c. Will this be the last such letter you will write?

UNFINISHED BUSINESS LETTER

The problems we face are sometimes the result of relationships that resulted in unfinished business. This can happen because one party or the other is unable or unwilling to resolve an issue at the time it arises. Frequently, such an issue can be satisfactorily reopened and resolved. This exercise presents one way to do that.

The exercise is to write a letter to the person with whom you feel you have unfinished business. You can use this sheet to get your thoughts together before writing the letter on a separate paper.

1. Write a factual account of the situation that caused the problem.

   _____

   _____

   _____

   _____

2. What haven't you said that you now might feel ready to say?

   _____

   _____

   _____

3. Explain your feelings about the problem.

   _____

   _____

   _____

4. What do you appreciate about what happened?

   _____

   _____

   _____

5. What do you not like about what happened?

   _____

   _____

   _____

6. List any regrets you have about the situation.

_____

_____

_____

7. Spell out clearly any wishes, demands, or requests you want to make.

_____

_____

_____

8. Is there anything else you want to include in the letter?

_____

_____

_____

After you have composed the letter, answer the following questions:

9. What do you want to do with the letter?

_____

_____

_____

10. If it can't be delivered or if it is better for you not to do so, list three things that you could do with the letter that might be meaningful to you.

    1. _____

    2. _____

    3. _____

Remember to bring completed work sheet to your next appointment

LOOK AT IT ANOTHER WAY

BREAK IT DOWN

GOALS OF THE EXERCISE

1. To suggest that there are other ways to see the problem.
2. To encourage the client to break the problem down into smaller elements or steps.
3. To help the client decide where to direct energy in making changes.

TYPES OF PROBLEMS THIS EXERCISE MAY BE MOST USEFUL FOR

- Adjustment disorder.
- Anger management.
- Anxiety.
- Chemical dependence/relapse.
- Childhood trauma.
- Dependency.
- Depression.
- Eating disorder.
- Family conflict.
- Impulse control disorder.
- Intimate relationship conflict.
- Low self-esteem.
- Phobia-panic/agoraphobia.
- Social discomfort.
- Type A behavior.
- Vocational stress.

SUGGESTIONS FOR PROCESSING THIS EXERCISE WITH CLIENT

a. What elements or steps make up the problem?
b. How can these elements be broken down?
c. Which are the most important elements?
d. Where is the best place to focus your energy?
e. Which elements would be a waste of your time to try to change?

BREAK IT DOWN

> It has been said that the best way to eat an elephant is one mouthful at a time. Problem solving is often similar in that progress becomes difficult if one is trying to do too much at once. Here is an exercise to help you break the problem into bite-size pieces.

1. If your problem had a recipe, what would be the ingredients? Take enough time to get them all and try to name at least five.

    1. _____
    2. _____
    3. _____
    4. _____
    5. _____

2. Divide each of these ingredients into at least two smaller elements or steps.

    1. _____   _____
    2. _____   _____
    3. _____   _____
    4. _____   _____
    5. _____   _____

3. Prioritize each of these elements or steps in order of their relative importance to the survival of the problem.

    1. _____   6. _____
    2. _____   7. _____
    3. _____   8. _____
    4. _____   9. _____
    5. _____   10. _____

4. Which five elements can you most easily control or influence?

    1. _____   4. _____
    2. _____   5. _____
    3. _____

5. Which five are most out of your control?

1. _____   4. _____

2. _____   5. _____

3. _____

6. For those elements that are beyond your control, what steps can you take to gain some control or influence over them?

_____

_____

_____

_____

_____

Remember to bring completed work sheet to your next appointment

PERSPECTIVE

GOALS OF THE EXERCISE

1. To place the problem in perspective.
2. To encourage the client to consider the ways that time and place influence understanding of the problem.
3. To suggest that there are many perspectives from which the problem can be seen.
4. To point out to the client that there is more to life than just the problem.

TYPES OF PROBLEMS THIS EXERCISE MAY BE MOST USEFUL FOR

- Adjustment disorder.
- Anxiety.
- Chemical dependence/relapse.
- Childhood trauma.
- Dependency.
- Depression.
- Family conflict.
- Grief/loss unresolved.
- Impulse control disorder.
- Intimate relationship conflict.
- Legal conflict.
- Low self-esteem.
- Obsessive-compulsive behavior.
- Phobia-panic/agoraphobia.
- Sleep disturbance.
- Social discomfort.
- Suicidal ideation.
- Type A behavior.
- Vocational stress.

SUGGESTIONS FOR PROCESSING THIS EXERCISE WITH CLIENT

a. How important is this problem in relation to the rest of your life?
b. How might you better spend your time rather than focusing on this problem?
c. What bearing did the location where you thought about your problem have on your thinking?

PERSPECTIVE

Space and time are major factors in determining how we understand our world. This exercise is designed to help you consider your situation from different viewpoints.

1. On a scale of 1 to 10, how important will this problem be in a month? _____ In a year? _____ In five years? _____

2. Explain why any changes in importance might occur.

_____

_____

_____

3. What are three more important issues or things in your life on which you can focus?

    1. _____

    2. _____

    3. _____

4. Go to the following places and think about your problem. What do you notice is different about the experience of thinking about the problem in these places?

    A playground

_____

_____

_____

    A church

_____

_____

_____

    A public park

_____

_____

_____

A mall

_____

_____

_____

An airport

_____

_____

_____

By a river, lake, or ocean

_____

_____

_____

While exercising

_____

_____

_____

A hospital

_____

_____

_____

A funeral home

_____

_____

_____

5. How does this problem influence your ability to do the work that gives your life meaning?

_____

_____

_____

Remember to bring completed work sheet to your next appointment

MULTIPLY EXPLANATIONS

GOALS OF THE EXERCISE

1. To challenge the client to create other explanations for the situation.
2. To encourage the client to consider the possibility that there can be more than one valid explanation for the situation.
3. To invite the client to consider the effects of one's beliefs.
4. To suggest that the client change his or her behavior.

TYPES OF PROBLEMS THIS EXERCISE MAY BE MOST USEFUL FOR

- Anger management.
- Antisocial behavior.
- Anxiety.
- Dependency.
- Depression.
- Family conflict.
- Impulse control disorder.
- Intimate relationship conflict.
- Low self-esteem.
- Obsessive-compulsive behavior.
- Paranoid ideation.
- Social discomfort.
- Vocational stress.

SUGGESTIONS FOR PROCESSING THIS EXERCISE WITH CLIENT

a. How do you usually think about the problem?
b. What are some other ways to think about the situation?
c. What would happen if you were to start thinking about the problem differently?
d. What would happen if you were to start acting differently?

MULTIPLY EXPLANATIONS

It's easy to think that your explanation for the problem is the only true explanation; however, there can be more than one way to see the situation, and keeping that in mind can be helpful. The purpose of this exercise is to help you broaden your vision.

1. Write your usual explanation for your problem.

   _____

   _____

   _____

2. Now write 10 other explanations. Be creative. Let your mind wander without censoring it. Don't rule out the influences of the stars, UFOs, or conspiracy theories.

   1. _____

   2. _____

   3. _____

   4. _____

   5. _____

   6. _____

   7. _____

   8. _____

   9. _____

   10. _____

3. Rule out the alternative explanations that a neutral person would judge to be less than 50 percent likely.

4. Of those remaining, which could account for your current situation as well as your original explanation does?

   _____

   _____

   _____

5. For each alternative explanation, list three ways that your behavior would change if you were to adopt that explanation.

    1. _____
    2. _____
    3. _____
    4. _____
    5. _____
    6. _____
    7. _____
    8. _____
    9. _____
    10. _____

6. For each behavior change in item 5, what would be the effect of simply changing your behavior in that way right now?

    1. _____
    2. _____
    3. _____
    4. _____
    5. _____
    6. _____
    7. _____
    8. _____
    9. _____
    10. _____

Remember to bring completed work sheet to your next appointment

FROM BLAME TO RESPONSIBILITY

GOALS OF THE EXERCISE

1. To suggest that there can be a distinction made between blame and responsibility.
2. To help the client identify whether blame or responsibility is being handed out.
3. To encourage the client to think about one's interactions with others.

TYPES OF PROBLEMS THIS EXERCISE MAY BE MOST USEFUL FOR

- Anger management.
- Antisocial behavior.
- Dependency.
- Depression.
- Family conflict.
- Intimate relationship conflict.
- Legal conflict.
- Low self-esteem.
- Suicidal ideation.

SUGGESTIONS FOR PROCESSING THIS EXERCISE WITH CLIENT

a. What do you see as the difference between blame and responsibility?
b. What are the positives and negatives of assigning blame and responsibility?
c. How do you go about assigning blame and responsibility?
d. How do people respond differently to blame and responsibility?

FROM BLAME TO RESPONSIBILITY

It is common to respond to problems by looking for someone or something to blame. This may not always be the best way to approach solving some of these problems. This exercise is designed to help you think about how you handle these situations.

1. What are your definitions of blame and responsibility?

   Blame: _____

   _____

   Responsibility: _____

   _____

2. How do you respond differently when you are blamed for something than when you are held responsible without being blamed?

   Blamed: _____

   _____

   Held responsible: _____

   _____

3. With what types of problems do you think assigning blame is a helpful strategy?

   _____

   _____

   _____

4. When are problems more easily solved by simply assigning responsibility?

   _____

   _____

   _____

5. List five or more words or phrases you could use when you are laying blame.

   1. _____
   2. _____
   3. _____
   4. _____
   5. _____

6. List five or more words or phrases you could use when assigning responsibility.

   1. _____
   2. _____
   3. _____
   4. _____
   5. _____

7. In looking over these words and phrases, which is more likely to gain your cooperation?

   _____
   _____
   _____
   _____

Remember to bring completed work sheet to your next appointment

Section VII

USE WHAT YOU'VE GOT

GO (SOMEWHAT) WITH THE FLOW

GOALS OF THE EXERCISE

1. To propose that nature has a flow of its own.
2. To suggest that the client can work with the natural flow to help achieve goals.

TYPES OF PROBLEMS THIS EXERCISE MAY BE MOST USEFUL FOR

- Adjustment disorder.
- Anger management.
- Antisocial behavior.
- Anxiety.
- Chemical dependence/relapse.
- Childhood trauma.
- Cognitive deficit.
- Dependency.
- Depression.
- Dissociation.
- Eating disorder.
- Educational deficit.
- Family conflict.
- Female sexual dysfunction.
- Grief/loss unresolved.
- Impulse control disorder.
- Intimate relationship conflict.
- Legal conflict.
- Low self-esteem.
- Male sexual dysfunction.
- Mania or hypomania.
- Medical issue.
- Obsessive-compulsive behavior.

- Paranoid ideation.
- Phobia-panic/agoraphobia.
- Psychoticism.
- Sexual abuse.
- Sleep disturbance.
- Social discomfort.
- Somatization.
- Spiritual confusion.
- Suicidal ideation.
- Type A behavior.
- Vocational stress.

SUGGESTIONS FOR PROCESSING THIS EXERCISE WITH CLIENT

a. How would you face the problem head-on?
b. What would happen?
c. What ideas did you try that were less direct?
d. Did they help?
e. What do you want to change or fine-tune?

GO (SOMEWHAT) WITH THE FLOW

A riptide flows away from the beach. A swimmer (A) who swims directly toward the beach will eventually become exhausted because the current of the riptide takes one away from the beach and out to sea. The way to escape is to swim parallel to the beach and away from the riptide (B). The riptide current will push you farther from shore at first, but you'll eventually swim out of the riptide and will then be able to return to shore.

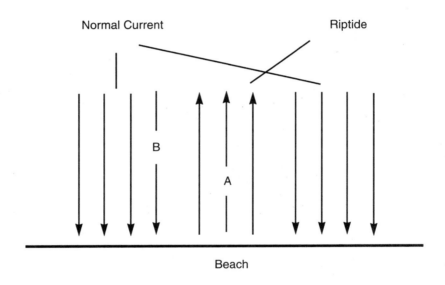

1. What forces are pushing you "out to sea"?

_____

_____

_____

2. If you were to face these forces head on, what would happen? If you have tried this approach in the past, what has happened?

_____

_____

_____

_____

_____

3. If you were to do nothing, what would happen?

_____

_____

_____

4. Reread the description of the riptide at the beginning of the exercise. Experiment with doing things that are less direct than facing the problem head-on, and don't give up. List your efforts below.

_____

_____

_____

_____

_____

5. What happened?

_____

_____

_____

_____

_____

Remember to bring completed work sheet to your next appointment

IDENTIFY AND VALIDATE FEELINGS

GOALS OF THE EXERCISE

1. To help the client stand apart from and think about his or her experience of feelings.
2. To challenge the idea that one is responsible for one's feelings.
3. To offer the idea that actions need not be determined by feelings.
4. To suggest that feelings can change.

TYPES OF PROBLEMS THIS EXERCISE MAY BE MOST USEFUL FOR

- Adjustment disorder.
- Anger management.
- Anxiety.
- Childhood trauma.
- Dependency.
- Depression.
- Eating disorder.
- Grief/loss unresolved.
- Intimate relationship conflict.
- Low self-esteem.
- Obsessive-compulsive behavior.
- Paranoid ideation.
- Phobia-panic/agoraphobia.
- Social discomfort.
- Suicidal ideation.
- Type A behavior.

SUGGESTIONS FOR PROCESSING THIS EXERCISE WITH CLIENT

a. What are your feelings and what is their importance?
b. What feelings can you control and what feelings are beyond your control?
c. How do feelings relate to behaviors?
d. What other feelings emerged when you allowed yourself to express your feeling with the name tag?

IDENTIFY AND VALIDATE FEELINGS

Feelings are an important part of our experience, but they can also sometimes be a source of problems. This exercise gives you some things to think about regarding your feelings and how you think about them.

1. List your feelings about the problem.

_____

_____

_____

_____

2. What is your reaction to having these feelings?

_____

_____

_____

3. What does it say about you that you have these feelings?

_____

_____

_____

4. Which of these feelings can you change at will?

_____

_____

_____

5. How do you explain the fact that sometimes you don't let your feelings gain complete control over your actions?

_____

_____

_____

6. When your feelings start to change, how will that affect your actions or your experience?

   _____

   _____

   _____

7. Write down one of the feelings that has been causing you trouble on a name tag and wear it under your clothes for a day. Throughout the day, consciously allow yourself to express the chosen feeling by focusing on the name tag and see what a difference that makes in your attitude. Repeat the exercise each day with a different feeling. Note any comments on your experience below.

   _____

   _____

   _____

   _____

   _____

Remember to bring completed work sheet to your next appointment

BUT, IT COULD HAPPEN

GOALS OF THE EXERCISE

1. To build rapport by joining the client in efforts being made toward solving the problem.
2. To remind the client that worries are a form of fantasy.
3. To introduce change in the client's behavior in the problem situation.

TYPES OF PROBLEMS THIS EXERCISE MAY BE MOST USEFUL FOR

- Adjustment disorder.
- Anger management.
- Antisocial behavior.
- Chemical dependence/relapse.
- Childhood trauma.
- Cognitive deficit.
- Dependency.
- Dissociation.
- Eating disorder.
- Educational deficit.
- Family conflict.
- Female sexual dysfunction.
- Grief/loss unresolved.
- Impulse control disorder.
- Intimate relationship conflict.
- Legal conflict.
- Low self-esteem.
- Male sexual dysfunction.
- Mania or hypomania.
- Medical issue.
- Paranoid ideation.
- Phobia-panic/agoraphobia.

- Psychoticism.
- Sexual abuse.
- Social discomfort.
- Somatization.
- Spiritual confusion.
- Suicidal ideation.
- Type A behavior.
- Vocational stress.

SUGGESTIONS FOR PROCESSING THIS EXERCISE WITH CLIENT

a. What was difficult about this exercise?
b. What do you think about that? Why were those things difficult for you?
c. What happened when you did this exercise?
d. What have you learned?

BUT, IT COULD HAPPEN

Think of this as an experiment. Every time you find yourself worrying about something that may not happen or over which you have no control, write down what it is about which you are worrying. Then identify three things that could happen that would be more serious. These three things must be dire; they ought to be just a bit short of Armageddon, but that might be one of them. Spend some time getting into each of the new disasters you concoct and try to realize you are making this up.

1. Original worry: _____

   New ideas:

   1. _____
   2. _____
   3. _____

2. Original worry: _____

   New ideas:

   1. _____
   2. _____
   3. _____

3. Original worry: _____

   New ideas:

   1. _____
   2. _____
   3. _____

4. Original worry: _____

   New ideas:

   1. _____
   2. _____
   3. _____

Remember to bring completed work sheet to your next appointment

Section VIII

GET A HANDLE ON THE PROBLEM

CHECK IT AT THE DOOR

GOAL OF THE EXERCISE

To suggest that the client can go on with the necessities of life before the problem is solved.

TYPES OF PROBLEMS THIS EXERCISE MAY BE MOST USEFUL FOR

- Anxiety.
- Depression.
- Obsessive-compulsive behavior.
- Phobia-panic/agoraphobia.
- Sleep disturbance.
- Social discomfort.

SUGGESTIONS FOR PROCESSING THIS EXERCISE WITH CLIENT

a. Where was this exercise helpful?
b. Did you make any changes that improved the exercise?

CHECK IT AT THE DOOR

As you enter a location where you need to be able to concentrate on something other than the difficulties you have been experiencing, look for a place to hang your problem. Find a specific spot or item such as a brick, doorknob, or shrub. Touch the object and feel the problem leave your body. While you are inside, if you think of the problem, think of it hanging where you left it. You may wonder how it's doing out there without you. On your way out, remember to pick it up and take it with you.

For each situation where you use this exercise, record the location where you left your problem. Rate on a scale of 1 to 10 your success at leaving the problem in that place. What was different about the times when you were more successful?

1. Where you left the problem: _____

   Your success rating: _____

   Comments: _____

   _____

   _____

2. Where you left the problem: _____

   Your success rating: _____

   Comments: _____

   _____

   _____

3. Where you left the problem: _____

   Your success rating: _____

   Comments: _____

   _____

   _____

Remember to bring completed work sheet to your next appointment

SPEAKING METAPHORICALLY

GOALS OF THE EXERCISE

1. To invite the client to see the problem in another light.
2. To suggest that the problem may have similarities to other parts of the client's life where he or she may have more expertise.
3. To encourage the client to transfer abilities from an area of competence to the problem situation.

TYPES OF PROBLEMS THIS EXERCISE MAY BE MOST USEFUL FOR

- Adjustment disorder.
- Anger management.
- Anxiety.
- Chemical dependence/relapse.
- Childhood trauma.
- Dependency.
- Depression.
- Dissociation.
- Eating disorder.
- Family conflict.
- Female sexual dysfunction.
- Grief/loss unresolved.
- Impulse control disorder.
- Intimate relationship conflict.
- Low self-esteem.
- Male sexual dysfunction.
- Mania or hypomania.
- Obsessive-compulsive behavior.
- Paranoid ideation.
- Phobia-panic/agoraphobia.
- Sleep disturbance.

- Social discomfort.
- Suicidal ideation.
- Type A behavior.
- Vocational stress.

SUGGESTIONS FOR PROCESSING THIS EXERCISE WITH CLIENT

a. What does the problem remind you of?
b. How would you respond if your metaphorical problem were literally the problem?
c. What skills can you bring to the problem situation from your metaphorical understanding?

SPEAKING METAPHORICALLY

You might remember from a high school literature class that a simile is a statement that compares one thing to something different, usually using the word *like* or *as* (e.g., "It's like trying to fill a bottomless pit"). Using a metaphor is a technique in which the speaker says that one thing is another (e.g., "The sky was a sea of gold"). Metaphors and similes can be powerful tools in finding new ways to approach a problem.

1. Make three similes or metaphors for your problem.

   1. It's like _____
   2. _____
   3. _____

2. For each metaphor or simile, imagine that it is literally true. What would you do in that case? For instance, if you had a bottomless pit, you might build a cover for it.

   1. _____
   2. _____
   3. _____

3. Imagine yourself doing the actions in your similes.

4. How can you modify your metaphorical solutions so they can have practical applications to your problem situation?

   1. _____
      _____
   2. _____
      _____
   3. _____
      _____

Remember to bring completed work sheet to your next appointment

PUT A LID ON IT

GOALS OF THE EXERCISE

1. To help the client find a way to express oneself while still accomplishing what the client feels he or she needs to do.
2. To build rapport by joining the client's efforts.

TYPES OF PROBLEMS THIS EXERCISE MAY BE MOST USEFUL FOR

- Adjustment disorder.
- Anger management.
- Antisocial behavior.
- Anxiety.
- Chemical dependence/relapse.
- Childhood trauma.
- Cognitive deficit.
- Dependency.
- Depression.
- Dissociation.
- Eating disorder.
- Educational deficit.
- Family conflict.
- Female sexual dysfunction.
- Grief/loss unresolved.
- Impulse control disorder.
- Intimate relationship conflict.
- Legal conflict.
- Low self-esteem.
- Male sexual dysfunction.
- Mania or hypomania.
- Medical issue.
- Obsessive-compulsive behavior.

- Paranoid ideation.
- Phobia-panic/agoraphobia.
- Psychoticism.
- Sexual abuse.
- Sleep disturbance.
- Social discomfort.
- Somatization.
- Spiritual confusion.
- Suicidal ideation.
- Type A behavior.
- Vocational stress.

SUGGESTIONS FOR PROCESSING THIS EXERCISE WITH CLIENT

a. What has slowed your progress?
b. Where did you keep the paper?
c. What were your reactions to doing this exercise?

PUT A LID ON IT

1. Make a list of the things you do or have that keep you from making progress. (Feel free to draw pictures or to use any other possible method you might find useful for expressing yourself.) Here are a few common negatives to get you started. Circle the ones that apply to you and add your own.

   Fear.   Prejudices.
   Self-criticism.   Biases.
   Predictions of failure.   Anger.
   Calling yourself names.   Focusing on failures/ignoring successes.

   _____   _____
   _____   _____
   _____   _____
   _____   _____

2. Put this paper in a safe place where you can find it at any time. Store the experiences you have been having that are not helpful along with this paper, realizing that you know where they are should you need them. For the time being, review your list daily and see if you need to add or delete any of the items.

3. When you find one of these issues causing you problems, remind yourself that you have it stored safely away and that you don't have to carry it around with you. Then proceed with what you need to do.

   Remember to bring completed work sheet to your next appointment

Section IX

DO SOMETHING DIFFERENT

TAKE A HIKE

GOALS OF THE EXERCISE

1. To encourage the client to take action.
2. To introduce change and stimulation.

TYPES OF PROBLEMS THIS EXERCISE MAY BE MOST USEFUL FOR

- Depression.
- Low self-esteem.
- Phobia-panic/agoraphobia.
- Type A behavior.

SUGGESTIONS FOR PROCESSING THIS EXERCISE WITH CLIENT

a. What themes did you choose for your walks? Why?
b. What did you learn?
c. If you missed a day, how do you explain that?

TAKE A HIKE

When you get in a rut, you often forget to look outside yourself, but that's where the new ideas are! Try this exercise as a way to start breaking old habits.

Take a walk every day. You can decide how far you want to walk, but each walk should have a theme of your choosing. Here are some suggestions, but you can make up your own.

Plants.   Junk.
Wildlife.   Buildings/architecture.
Weather.   Sculpture.
People.   Fungi.
Sidewalks.   Colors.

As you walk each day, experience and learn three new things about your theme. Note those things below:

Day 1

    1. _____

    2. _____

    3. _____

Day 2

    1. _____

    2. _____

    3. _____

Day 3

    1. _____

    2. _____

    3. _____

Day 4

    1. _____

    2. _____

    3. _____

Day 5

   1. _____

   2. _____

   3. _____

Day 6

   1. _____

   2. _____

   3. _____

Day 7

   1. _____

   2. _____

   3. _____

Remember to bring completed work sheet to your next appointment

SOME DAYS ARE ODD

GOALS OF THE EXERCISE

1. To suggest that the client has some control over the situation.
2. To introduce some changes into the situation.
3. To dissuade the client from changing everything at once.

TYPES OF PROBLEMS THIS EXERCISE MAY BE MOST USEFUL FOR

- Anger management.
- Chemical dependence/relapse.
- Dependency.
- Dissociation.
- Eating disorder.
- Family conflict.
- Grief/loss unresolved.
- Impulse control disorder.
- Intimate relationship conflict.
- Low self-esteem.
- Obsessive-compulsive behavior.
- Paranoid ideation.
- Phobia-panic/agoraphobia.
- Sexual abuse.
- Type A behavior.

SUGGESTIONS FOR PROCESSING THIS EXERCISE WITH CLIENT

a. What do you want to change?
b. What is it that you would rather be doing?
c. What did you learn by keeping your old behavior?
d. What did you learn on the days you tried something different?
e. What difference will this make in the long run?

SOME DAYS ARE ODD

Sometimes when you find change is difficult it can be helpful to learn a bit more about a behavior before actually changing it. Here is one way to do that.

1. Write down the name of the behavior you want to change.

   _____

2. What would you rather be doing?

   _____

   _____

3. On odd-numbered days (e.g., the first and third of the month), do nothing different. Make those days exactly like the days you have been having. For each day, answer the questions below:

   Odd day: What did you do that was the same old thing? _____
   Observations and comments: _____

   _____

   Odd day: What did you do that was the same old thing? _____
   Observations and comments: _____

   _____

   Odd day: What did you do that was the same old thing? _____
   Observations and comments: _____

   _____

   Odd day: What did you do that was the same old thing? _____
   Observations and comments: _____

   _____

   Odd day: What did you do that was the same old thing? _____
   Observations and comments: _____

   _____

   Odd day: What did you do that was the same old thing? _____
   Observations and comments: _____

4. On even-numbered days, try the new behavior. For each day, answer the questions below:

Even day: What did you do that was different? _____
Observations and comments: _____

_____

Even day: What did you do that was different? _____
Observations and comments: _____

_____

Even day: What did you do that was different? _____
Observations and comments: _____

_____

Even day: What did you do that was different? _____
Observations and comments: _____

_____

Even day: What did you do that was different? _____
Observations and comments: _____

_____

Even day: What did you do that was different? _____
Observations and comments: _____

_____

Remember to bring completed work sheet to your next appointment

CHOREOGRAPH AN ARGUMENT

GOALS OF THE EXERCISE

1. To encourage the client to slow down and think.
2. To suggest specific changes that help in discussing differences.

TYPES OF PROBLEMS THIS EXERCISE MAY BE MOST USEFUL FOR

- Anger management.
- Antisocial behavior.
- Chemical dependence/relapse.
- Dependency.
- Depression.
- Family conflict.
- Female sexual dysfunction.
- Intimate relationship conflict.
- Low self-esteem.
- Male sexual dysfunction.
- Sexual abuse.

SUGGESTIONS FOR PROCESSING THIS EXERCISE WITH CLIENT

a. What helped?
b. What did you find outside the suggestions on the assignment sheet that helped?
c. What was difficult and how did you deal with it?

I would recommend discussing this exercise thoroughly with clients before sending them home to try it out. For a more thorough explanation of the ideas behind this exercise, read *Rewriting Love Stories*, by Pat Hudson and Bill O'Hanlon.

CHOREOGRAPH AN ARGUMENT

> Arguments that cause problems often take place because emotional people try to get their way. This exercise provides a framework for keeping the discussion focused on the behaviors you want to change.

1. Stop and think.

2. Exactly what happened that you didn't like? Put it in terms of who did what. Avoid blaming, labeling, or analyzing why they did it. Write a description of the incident or behavior below in item 7.

3. Do you need to talk about it or is it something that can be overlooked?

   _____

   _____

   _____

4. Is it something that the other person can do something about?

   _____

   _____

   _____

5. What do you want? Again, make very clear what you are asking for. Write it in item 8.

6. Find a time and place to talk when you can both give your full attention to the issue at hand.

7. Present the complaint.

   _____

   _____

8. Present one or more suggestions or requests.

    _____

    _____

    _____

9. Negotiate. While you are negotiating, remember:

    - That you are creating a solution that everyone can accept.
    - To keep looking for a solution to the original problem.
    - That you can take a time-out.
    - To listen and be sure that you understand what has been said before you prepare a response.
    - Not to give in just to end the argument.
    - To be sure you can and will do what you agree on.
    - To hold firmly to your values while remaining flexible on how you exemplify them.

10. Is the other person willing and able to do what was requested?

    _____

11. If not, brainstorm possible solutions. Without censoring them, write as many ideas for solutions that you can come up with.

    _____

    _____

    _____

    _____

12. Continue to negotiate for as long as it takes to come up with a solution acceptable to all concerned. Take breaks or days off as necessary. Keep the discussion focused on behavior that will solve the problem.

13. What specific action will be taken? When? By whom?

    _____

    _____

    _____

14. When will you review your progress?

    _____

15. The complainant will be on the lookout for any sign of progress or effort that the other person makes regarding the problem. Watch for the times the person does what he or she has agreed to do. Record the dates and times. At the time of the action, acknowledge the behavior to the person making the effort.

Date: _____ Time: _____   Date: _____ Time: _____

Date: _____ Time: _____   Date: _____ Time: _____

Date: _____ Time: _____   Date: _____ Time: _____

Remember to bring completed work sheet to your next appointment

FAKE IT 'TIL YOU MAKE IT

GOALS OF THE EXERCISE

1. To encourage the client to do something.
2. To suggest that the client can feel one way and act another.
3. To invite the client to lighten up.

TYPES OF PROBLEMS THIS EXERCISE MAY BE MOST USEFUL FOR

- Adjustment disorder.
- Anger management.
- Antisocial behavior.
- Anxiety.
- Chemical dependence/relapse.
- Childhood trauma.
- Cognitive deficit.
- Dependency.
- Depression.
- Eating disorder.
- Educational deficit.
- Family conflict.
- Grief/loss unresolved.
- Impulse control disorder.
- Intimate relationship conflict.
- Low self-esteem.
- Mania or hypomania.
- Medical issue.
- Obsessive-compulsive behavior.
- Paranoid ideation.
- Phobia-panic/agoraphobia.
- Psychoticism.
- Sexual abuse.

- Social discomfort.
- Somatization.
- Spiritual confusion.
- Suicidal ideation.
- Type A behavior.
- Vocational stress.

SUGGESTIONS FOR PROCESSING THIS EXERCISE WITH CLIENT

a. When has the problem typically happened?
b. If the problem were solved, how would you be acting differently?
c. What happened when you acted differently?
d. What did you learn?

FAKE IT 'TIL YOU MAKE IT

You may have observed that doing the same thing over and over tends to maintain the status quo. Getting out of that kind of rut may require a bold move. This exercise invites you to do that.

1. List five occasions where your problem typically influences your behavior.

    1. _____
    2. _____
    4. _____
    5. _____

2. Imagine you don't have the problem. List at least six specific things you would be doing differently in your everyday life.

    1. _____
    2. _____
    4. _____
    5. _____
    6. _____

3. Between now and your next session (at least once a day) act as if you don't have a problem. Fake it. Remember, you're just trying out a new behavior like you would try on a new suit of clothes. (Don't do anything that violates the law or your morals.)

4. What were the advantages and disadvantages of acting out your new behavior in each situation?

    Day 1
    Advantages: _____
    Disadvantages: _____

    Day 2
    Advantages: _____
    Disadvantages: _____

Day 3
Advantages: _____
Disadvantages: _____

Day 4
Advantages: _____
Disadvantages: _____

Day 5
Advantages: _____
Disadvantages: _____

Day 6
Advantages: _____
Disadvantages: _____

Day 7
Advantages: _____
Disadvantages: _____

Just before your next session, answer these questions:

5. What was difficult about doing this?

_____
_____
_____

6. How did others react?

_____
_____
_____

7. What surprised you about your new behavior?

_____
_____
_____

8. Would you like to continue your new behavior?

_____

Remember to bring completed work sheet to your next appointment

LETTER TO THE PROBLEM

GOALS OF THE EXERCISE

1. To externalize the problem.
2. To build rapport by joining the client's efforts.
3. To encourage acceptance and acknowledgement of one's own feelings.

TYPES OF PROBLEMS THIS EXERCISE MAY BE MOST USEFUL FOR

- Adjustment disorder.
- Anger management.
- Antisocial behavior.
- Anxiety.
- Chemical dependence/relapse.
- Childhood trauma.
- Cognitive deficit.
- Dependency.
- Depression.
- Dissociation.
- Eating disorder.
- Educational deficit.
- Family conflict.
- Female sexual dysfunction.
- Grief/loss unresolved.
- Impulse control disorder.
- Intimate relationship conflict.
- Legal conflict.
- Low self-esteem.
- Male sexual dysfunction.
- Mania or hypomania.
- Medical issue.
- Obsessive-compulsive behavior.

- Paranoid ideation.
- Phobia-panic/agoraphobia.
- Psychoticism.
- Sexual abuse.
- Sleep disturbance.
- Social discomfort.
- Somatization.
- Spiritual confusion.
- Suicidal ideation.
- Type A behavior.
- Vocational stress.

SUGGESTIONS FOR PROCESSING THIS EXERCISE WITH CLIENT

a. How did this exercise change the way you think about the problem?
b. What did you learn that might be helpful in dealing with the problem?
c. What was it like being the problem?

LETTER TO THE PROBLEM

1. On a separate sheet, write a letter to your problem. You could include:

   - How you see the situation.
   - Your feelings about the problem.
   - What you want from the problem.
   - The consequences of not getting what you want.
   - Anything else you like.

2. Be the problem and write a response to the issues raised in the letter.

3. Write another letter to the problem in response to what the problem has told you.

4. How was being the problem different from just being yourself?

   _____

   _____

   _____

5. How did your first and second letters to the problem differ?

   _____

   _____

   _____

   _____

6. What did you learn from this exercise?

   _____

   _____

   _____

   _____

Remember to bring completed work sheet to your next appointment

DO SOMETHING MORE DIFFERENT

BREAKING OUT

GOALS OF THE EXERCISE

1. To encourage the client to examine his or her assumptions.
2. To challenge the client to break out of self-imposed limitations.

TYPES OF PROBLEMS THIS EXERCISE MAY BE MOST USEFUL FOR

- Adjustment disorder.
- Anxiety.
- Chemical dependence/relapse.
- Childhood trauma.
- Cognitive deficit.
- Dependency.
- Depression.
- Educational deficit.
- Family conflict.
- Intimate relationship conflict.
- Low self-esteem.
- Obsessive-compulsive behavior.
- Phobia-panic/agoraphobia.
- Sleep disturbance.
- Social discomfort.
- Suicidal ideation.
- Type A behavior.
- Vocational stress.

SUGGESTIONS FOR PROCESSING THIS EXERCISE WITH CLIENT

a. What assumptions kept you from solving this puzzle?
b. What assumptions are you making in your problem situation?

c. What ideas do you have that would allow you to break out of your old patterns of attempting to solve the problem?

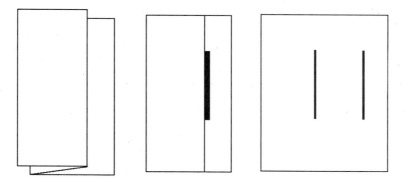

The key to solving the problem requires drawing two lines at once. You can do this by folding the paper and drawing a line in a way that the pencil marks a line on the flat paper and on the crease at the same time. When you unfold the paper, you will have two lines and can easily finish the exercise.

BREAKING OUT ·

Using a pencil and piece of paper, draw this figure without lifting the pencil or retracing a line. Anything else goes.

1. What assumptions did you make that kept you from immediately seeing the solution?

   _____

   _____

   _____

2. What are five assumptions you are making about your problem situation?
   1. _____
   2. _____
   3. _____
   4. _____
   5. _____

3. How do these assumptions limit your search for a solution to your problem?

   _____

   _____

   _____

   _____

   _____

4. As you get ideas about solving your problem that fly in the face of your old assumptions, list them below:

   _____

   _____

   _____

   _____

Remember to bring completed work sheet to your next appointment

YOU BET YOUR LIFE

GOALS OF THE EXERCISE

1. To introduce humor.
2. To make it difficult to repeat the problem behavior.

TYPES OF PROBLEMS THIS EXERCISE MAY BE MOST USEFUL FOR

- Anger management.
- Anxiety.
- Family conflict.

SUGGESTIONS FOR PROCESSING THIS EXERCISE WITH CLIENT

a. What difference did the glasses make?
b. What have you learned from this?

YOU BET YOUR LIFE

Purchase a pair of "Groucho" glasses for everyone typically involved in the problem pattern. At the first sign that the problem is appearing, everyone should put on their glasses, then proceed as usual. In the space below, note the dates and times that you do this exercise, as well as what happened.

1. Date: _____   Time: _____

    Who remembered to put on the glasses?

    _____

    What tipped them off that it was the right time?

    _____
    _____
    _____

    What difference did the glasses make? (Get everyone's ideas.)

    _____
    _____
    _____

2. Date: _____   Time: _____

    Who remembered to put on the glasses?

    _____

    What tipped them off that it was the right time?

    _____
    _____
    _____

    What difference did the glasses make? (Get everyone's ideas.)

    _____
    _____
    _____

Remember to bring completed work sheet to your next appointment

TRADING SIDES

GOALS OF THE EXERCISE

1. To encourage the listening to and understanding of the other person's position.
2. To suggest that there can be more than one valid way of seeing the situation.

TYPES OF PROBLEMS THIS EXERCISE MAY BE MOST USEFUL FOR

- Family conflict.
- Intimate relationship conflict.

SUGGESTIONS FOR PROCESSING THIS EXERCISE WITH CLIENT

a. How did you know it was time to do the exercise?
b. What was difficult about doing the exercise?
c. How did you know the other person understood you?
d. What did you learn from this exercise?

TRADING SIDES

Sometimes in a disagreement you get the idea that there is too much talk and not enough listening. This is an exercise that you can do when you feel unheard or misunderstood in a conversation.

The next time you find yourselves stuck in a disagreement, each of you should answer the following questions:

1. What are you asking for?

   _____

   _____

   _____

2. Why are these things important?

   _____

   _____

   _____

3. Trade chairs or locations and argue the other person's points as passionately as you argued your own. Set a timer and talk for five minutes.

4. Return to your original positions and continue your discussion for another five minutes.

5. Continue to trade positions every five minutes until you are satisfied that you each feel understood.

6. How long did it take for you to convince each other you were listening?

   _____

7. What did you learn about the other person's position?

   _____

   _____

   _____

8. What difference did it make in your discussion?

_____

_____

_____

Suggestion: You can do this exercise as many times as you need to.

Remember to bring completed work sheet to your next appointment

TURN THAT NOISE DOWN

GOALS OF THE EXERCISE

1. To build rapport by joining the client's efforts.
2. To suggest a change.
3. To propose that the client has some influence in the problem situation.

TYPES OF PROBLEMS THIS EXERCISE MAY BE MOST USEFUL FOR

- Adjustment disorder.
- Anger management.
- Anxiety.
- Dependency.
- Depression.
- Low self-esteem.
- Obsessive-compulsive behavior.
- Paranoid ideation.
- Social discomfort.
- Suicidal ideation.

SUGGESTIONS FOR PROCESSING THIS EXERCISE WITH CLIENT

a. Which voice was helpful?
b. What happened when you did this exercise?
c. What do you make of the result?
d. How could you use this experience to help you with the problem?

TURN THAT NOISE DOWN

Inner voices can sometimes become very annoying. You may not be able to turn them off or to simply ignore them, but sometimes you can change them so they're not so bothersome.

You can do these activities out loud or internally:

1. Repeat the thought three times in fast motion so that it sounds like chipmunks.
2. Say the thought three times very slowly.
3. Shout the thought three times.
4. Whisper the thought three times so it is barely audible.
5. Choose you favorite voice from the movies and say the thought three times in that voice.
6. Now repeat the thought one time in your normal voice.

Each time you do this exercise answer the following questions:

1. Date: _____ Time: _____

   What voice did you choose?

   _____

   When you repeated the thought was it more or less annoying than when you started?

   _____

2. Date: _____ Time: _____

   What voice did you choose?

   _____

   When you repeated the thought was it more or less annoying than when you started?

   _____

3. Date: _____ Time: _____

   What voice did you choose?

   _____

   When you repeated the thought was it more or less annoying than when you started?

   _____

4. Date: _____ Time: _____

   What voice did you choose?

   _____

   When you repeated the thought was it more or less annoying than when you started?

   _____

5. Date: _____ Time: _____

   What voice did you choose?

   _____

   When you repeated the thought was it more or less annoying than when you started?

   _____

6. Date: _____ Time: _____

   What voice did you choose?

   _____

   When you repeated the thought was it more or less annoying than when you started?

   _____

Remember to bring completed work sheet to your next appointment

Section XI

MAKE A CHOICE

CHOOSING A LOVER

GOALS OF THE EXERCISE

1. To encourage the client to think before making an important decision.
2. To suggest certain subjects for the client to think about.

TYPES OF PROBLEMS THIS EXERCISE MAY BE MOST USEFUL FOR

- Intimate relationship conflict.
- Low self-esteem.
- Spiritual confusion.

SUGGESTIONS FOR PROCESSING THIS EXERCISE WITH CLIENT

a. Which items do you find give you cause for concern?
b. What traits mentioned in the exercise do you think are unimportant?
c. What characteristics of the other person do you need more data about?
d. How will you get that information?

CHOOSING A LOVER

Most of us are guided more by feelings than by logic when we make choices about with whom we want to become intimately involved. If you have a history of making poor choices, perhaps a little more thinking would help you in the future. Some factors that are commonly accepted as being important in relationships are listed below. For each trait, rate your confidence that you and the other person can get along from 1 to 10, with 1 being the lowest. Then write the evidence you have for your confidence or for the things your lover has done that cause you concern.

1. Accepts responsibility for own actions. Rating ___

   Comments:

   _____

   _____

   _____

2. Respects your opinions and feelings. Rating ___

   Comments:

   _____

   _____

   _____

3. Tolerates differences between the two of you. Rating ___

   Comments:

   _____

   _____

   _____

4. Tells the truth. Rating ___

   Comments:

   _____

   _____

   _____

5. Follows through on commitments. Rating ___

   Comments:

   _____

   _____

   _____

6. Respects your freedom of movement and right to socialize. Rating ___

   Comments:

   _____

   _____

   _____

7. Respects your privacy and your property. Rating ___

   Comments:

   _____

   _____

   _____

8. Accepts things about you that you can't control (e.g., your emotions or wishes) or that are none of his or her business (e.g., your looks or weight). Rating ___

   Comments:

   _____

   _____

   _____

9. Is willing and able to appropriately express his or her needs and desires. Rating ___

   Comments:

   _____

   _____

   _____

10. Has sexual attitudes and expectations that are compatible with yours. Rating ___

    Comments:

    _____

    _____

    _____

11. Has attitudes about children that are compatible with yours (number, timing, discipline, etc.). Rating ___

    Comments:

    _____

    _____

    _____

12. Has attitudes about drugs, alcohol, gambling, etc., that are compatible with yours. Rating ___

    Comments:

    _____

    _____

    _____

13. Demonstrates responsible money management. Rating ___

    Comments:

    _____

    _____

    _____

14. Has religious and/or cultural beliefs that are compatible with yours. Rating ___

    Comments:

    _____

    _____

    _____

15. Does his or her share of the work. Rating ___

    Comments:

    _____

    _____

    _____

16. Gets along with your family and you get along with his or hers. Rating ___

    Comments:

    _____

    _____

    _____

17. Is respectful of your career and you are comfortable with the way he or she handles own work. Rating ___

    Comments:

    _____

    _____

    _____

18. Is in good physical health or has no illness or disability that is cause for concern. Rating ___

    Comments:

    _____

    _____

    _____

Feel free to add other items that are important to you.

Suggestion: If you find that you are concerned about an area that is important to you, get it straightened out before making a serious commitment. Don't assume that things will change for the better on their own.

Remember to bring completed work sheet to your next appointment

JUST IMAGINE

GOALS OF THE EXERCISE

1. To remind clients that decisions are made with incomplete knowledge.
2. To challenge the client to create different options.
3. To encourage the client to get specific about expectations.

TYPES OF PROBLEMS THIS EXERCISE MAY BE MOST USEFUL FOR

- Intimate relationship conflict.
- Spiritual confusion.
- Vocational stress.

SUGGESTIONS FOR PROCESSING THIS EXERCISE WITH CLIENT

a. What options do you see?
b. What do you think are the possible effects of each?
c. Which decision will best help you fulfill your life's work?

JUST IMAGINE

As far as we can tell, no one can know the future; however, we all have to make decisions based on our best guesses about what will happen. Here is an exercise to help you clarify what you know and what you think might happen.

1. List three possible options you see before you.

    1. _____
    2. _____
    3. _____

Imagine yourself five years from now having taken one of the options you are currently contemplating. Let your imagination go and put yourself five years into the future as you answer the following questions.

2. Where do you live and how do you feel about it?

    _____

    _____

    _____

3. How do you spend your time and how do you feel about it?

    _____

    _____

    _____

4. Describe your relationships with five of the important people in your life.

    1. _____
    2. _____
    3. _____
    4. _____
    5. _____

5. How did your decision five years ago affect your life?

    _____

    _____

    _____

6. What was difficult about making that decision and seeing it through?

_____

_____

_____

7. How did others react?

_____

_____

_____

8. Where did you get the strength to do what you felt you needed to do?

_____

_____

_____

9. Did your decision make you more or less able to do what you think is important in life?

_____

_____

_____

10. In what ways do you like your life more now than you liked it five years ago?

_____

_____

_____

_____

11. Do you have any regrets?

_____

_____

_____

_____

Repeat this exercise with each of the options you see for yourself.

Remember to bring completed work sheet to your next appointment

YEA OR NAY?

GOALS OF THE EXERCISE

1. To suggest that in difficult situations, no solution is perfect.
2. To encourage the client to consider alternatives in light of personal values.
3. To point out that negative aspects can sometimes be dealt with.

TYPES OF PROBLEMS THIS EXERCISE MAY BE MOST USEFUL FOR

- Adjustment disorder.
- Anxiety.
- Dependency.
- Family conflict.
- Intimate relationship conflict.
- Legal conflict.
- Vocational stress.

SUGGESTIONS FOR PROCESSING THIS EXERCISE WITH CLIENT

a. What are your alternatives?
b. What have you learned from this exercise?

Section XII

TAKE CARE OF YOURSELF

DEFINE THE RELATIONSHIP

GOALS OF THE EXERCISE

1. To help the client clarify expectations for self and for the other.
2. To encourage the client to share expectations with the other.
3. To invite the client to see communication as a statement of the relationship.

TYPES OF PROBLEMS THIS EXERCISE MAY BE MOST USEFUL FOR

- Anger management.
- Dependency.
- Depression.
- Family conflict.
- Intimate relationship conflict.
- Low self-esteem.
- Vocational stress.

SUGGESTIONS FOR PROCESSING THIS EXERCISE WITH CLIENT

a. What do you expect from the other person?
b. Have you shared these expectations with the other person?
c. What effect do you think sharing them would have?

DEFINE THE RELATIONSHIP

Have you ever clarified what you expect from the other person involved in your relationship? Making your expectations clear to yourself and to others can make a difference.

1. List the roles you expect the person to fill for you (e.g., lover, chauffeur, parent to your kids). For each role, list in detail the things the person would need to do for you to make you feel that he or she has fulfilled that role.

   Role 1

   _____

   Expectations

   _____

   _____

   _____

   Role 2

   _____

   Expectations

   _____

   _____

   _____

   Role 3

   _____

   Expectations

   _____

   _____

   _____

   Role 4

   _____

Expectations

_____

_____

_____

Role 5

_____

Expectations

_____

_____

_____

2. Look over your list to be sure that your expectations are crystal clear. Be sure they state specifically what the person will do rather than what qualities he or she will have (e.g., rather than wanting a person to be responsible, you might want him or her to balance the checkbook each month). Rephrase the expectations if necessary.

3. Do you think your expectations are reasonable?

_____

4. Are you willing to share this belief with the person?

_____

5. Does that make it more or less likely that you will get what you want?

_____

6. What does that say about your relationship?

_____

_____

_____

7. How do you think this will this affect your future behavior?

_____

_____

_____

Remember to bring completed work sheet to your next appointment

SELFISH OR SELF-SUFFICIENT?

GOALS OF THIS EXERCISE

1. To imply that the client sometimes does take care of himself or herself.
2. To help the client distinguish between being selfish and taking care of oneself.
3. To suggest that the client can take care of self even if it feels uncomfortable.

TYPES OF PROBLEMS THIS EXERCISE MAY BE MOST USEFUL FOR

- Anxiety.
- Dependency.
- Depression.
- Family conflict.
- Intimate relationship conflict.
- Low self-esteem.

SUGGESTIONS FOR PROCESSING THIS EXERCISE WITH CLIENT

a. How do you take care of yourself?
b. What's the difference between taking care of yourself and being selfish?
c. What prevents you from taking care of yourself?
d. How do you sometimes take care of yourself in spite of the fact that it might make you feel uncomfortable to do so?

SELFISH OR SELF-SUFFICIENT?

It's common knowledge that you need to take care of yourself, but at the same time, we're often told not to be selfish. Knowing the difference between the two states can be difficult, but it is important to see what distinguishes one from the other.

1. Name five things you do to take care of yourself.

    1. _____
    2. _____
    3. _____
    4. _____
    5. _____

2. How many of these things do you feel are selfish acts?

    _____

3. What do you think is the difference between taking care of yourself and being selfish?

    Taking care of myself is . . .

    _____

    _____

    _____

    Being selfish is . . .

    _____

    _____

    _____

4. If you don't take care of yourself, who does?

    _____

5. What has stopped you from taking care of yourself in the past?

    _____

    _____

    _____

6. How do you sometimes and in some circumstances do things to take care of yourself in spite of the fact that you or others may feel that you are being selfish?

   _____

   _____

   _____

7. Between now and your next appointment, notice the times you are forced to decide between doing something for yourself and doing something that someone else would prefer. Ask yourself, "If I were to do this, would I be taking care of myself or would I be acting selfishly?" Record your experiences below.

   _____

   _____

   _____

   _____

   _____

Remember to bring completed work sheet to your next appointment

WHAT DO YOU NEED?

GOALS OF THE EXERCISE

1. To help the client to clearly identify needs.
2. To point out that the client is responsible for fulfilling own needs.
3. To suggest that the client can take care of himself or herself even if it feels uncomfortable.

TYPES OF PROBLEMS THIS EXERCISE MAY BE MOST USEFUL FOR

- Adjustment disorder.
- Anxiety.
- Dependency.
- Depression.
- Intimate relationship conflict.
- Low self-esteem.
- Suicidal ideation.
- Vocational stress.

SUGGESTIONS FOR PROCESSING THIS EXERCISE WITH CLIENT

a. What do you need?
b. What keeps you from meeting your needs?
c. How do you know you are not getting what you need?
d. What happens when you take care of yourself?

WHAT DO YOU NEED?

1. What do you think you need and deserve, just by by virtue of the fact that you are a member of the human race?

   Physical needs:

   _____
   _____
   _____
   _____

   Emotional needs:

   _____
   _____
   _____
   _____

2. What might keep you from doing that which is necessary to get your needs met?

   _____
   _____
   _____

3. What are your clues that your needs are not being met or that someone is taking advantage of you?

   Physical sensations:

   _____
   _____
   _____

   Thoughts:

   _____
   _____
   _____

Feelings:

_____

_____

_____

4. Between now and your next session, identify five or more times when you step out of your comfort zone in order to get your needs met. Briefly describe those experiences below so you can discuss them in your next session.

   1. _____

   2. _____

   3. _____

   4. _____

   5. _____

5. What was difficult about doing these things?

_____

_____

_____

_____

_____

6. How did you get yourself to do what was necessary?

_____

_____

_____

_____

_____

Remember to bring completed work sheet to your next appointment

WHAT'S YOUR PLEASURE?

GOALS OF THE EXERCISE

1. To point out that the client has the ability to get in touch with oneself.
2. To prepare for future difficulties.
3. To encourage the client to take care of himself or herself.

TYPES OF PROBLEMS THIS EXERCISE MAY BE MOST USEFUL FOR

- Dependency.
- Depression.
- Family conflict.
- Intimate relationship conflict.
- Low self-esteem.

SUGGESTIONS FOR PROCESSING THIS EXERCISE WITH CLIENT

a. What can you do to take care of yourself?
b. How can you best use this information?

WHAT'S YOUR PLEASURE?

When you are under stress it can be difficult to remember that you also have the ability to relax and to take care of yourself. For this exercise, notice the things that help you get in touch with yourself. Look for things that make you feel good about yourself, confident, and worthwhile. Keep this list handy and refer to it when you need some ideas for ways to take care of yourself. Sometimes just thinking about these things can help you calm down in a situation.

1. What relaxing activities do you enjoy?

    _____

    _____

    _____

2. What are some physical pleasures that make you feel good about yourself?

    _____

    _____

    _____

3. What are some places to go that help you get in touch with yourself?

    _____

    _____

    _____

4. Who are the people whose company you enjoy and who make you feel worth-while?

    _____

    _____

    _____

5. What material items give you confidence?

    _____

    _____

    _____

Remember to bring completed work sheet to your next appointment

Section XIII

CLARIFY VALUES

WHY ARE YOU HERE?

GOALS OF THE EXERCISE

1. To encourage the client to create meaning in his or her life.
2. To suggest that meaning can be found in everyday activities.

TYPES OF PROBLEMS THIS EXERCISE MAY BE MOST USEFUL FOR

- Anxiety.
- Depression.
- Spiritual confusion.

SUGGESTIONS FOR PROCESSING THIS EXERCISE WITH CLIENT

a. What do you think people think of you?
b. What would you like people to think about you?
c. What impact do you have on your world?
d. What would you like to do differently?
e. When did you notice you were feeling that you were doing something meaningful?

WHY ARE YOU HERE?

It's easy to get caught up in everyday activities and to lose track of the big picture. When this happens, petty difficulties can seem to take on galactic proportions and decisions can become extremely difficult. Here are some suggestions for things to think about to help you keep things in perspective.

1. List the 10 most important people in your life and how they would remember you if you were to leave the planet today.

   1. _____
   2. _____
   3. _____
   4. _____
   5. _____
   6. _____
   7. _____
   8. _____
   9. _____
   10. _____

2. How would you like to be remembered by these people?

   _____
   _____
   _____
   _____
   _____

3. What are 10 ways that the world is different because you existed?

   1. _____
   2. _____
   3. _____
   4. _____
   5. _____
   6. _____

7. _____

8. _____

9. _____

10. _____

4. Write 10 things you feel are important for you to change.

    1. _____

    2. _____

    3. _____

    4. _____

    5. _____

    6. _____

    7. _____

    8. _____

    9. _____

    10. _____

5. Between now and your next session, list the events that made you feel that you were doing something worthwhile.

    _____

    _____

    _____

    _____

Remember to bring completed work sheet to your next appointment

WHAT DO YOU DO?

GOAL OF THE EXERCISE

To encourage the client to examine how one's time is spent and analyze that in regard to personal values.

TYPES OF PROBLEMS THIS EXERCISE MAY BE MOST USEFUL FOR

- Family conflict.
- Intimate relationship conflict.
- Spiritual confusion.
- Vocational stress.

SUGGESTIONS FOR PROCESSING THIS EXERCISE WITH CLIENT

a. What do you think about how you spend your time?
b. What values are reflected by the ways in which you choose to use your time?
c. Tell me about the values you want to demonstrate more.
d. How do you want to change your behavior?

WHAT DO YOU DO?

1. Track your daily activity for an entire week. Be as specific as you can.

Day 1

   7:00 _____

   8:00 _____

   9:00 _____

  10:00 _____

  11:00 _____

  12:00 _____

   1:00 _____

   2:00 _____

   3:00 _____

   4:00 _____

   5:00 _____

   6:00 _____

   7:00 _____

   8:00 _____

   9:00 _____

  10:00 _____

  11:00 _____

  12:00 _____

Day 2

   7:00 _____

   8:00 _____

   9:00 _____

  10:00 _____

  11:00 _____

  12:00 _____

   1:00 _____

   2:00 _____

   3:00 _____

4:00 _____

5:00 _____

6:00 _____

7:00 _____

8:00 _____

9:00 _____

10:00 _____

11:00 _____

12:00 _____

Day 3

7:00 _____

8:00 _____

9:00 _____

10:00 _____

11:00 _____

12:00 _____

1:00 _____

2:00 _____

3:00 _____

4:00 _____

5:00 _____

6:00 _____

7:00 _____

8:00 _____

9:00 _____

10:00 _____

11:00 _____

12:00 _____

Day 4

7:00 _____

8:00 _____

9:00 _____

10:00 _____

11:00 _____

12:00 _____

1:00 _____

2:00 _____

3:00 _____

4:00 _____

5:00 _____

6:00 _____

7:00 _____

8:00 _____

9:00 _____

10:00 _____

11:00 _____

12:00 _____

Day 5

7:00 _____

8:00 _____

9:00 _____

10:00 _____

11:00 _____

12:00 _____

1:00 _____

2:00 _____

3:00 _____

4:00 _____

5:00 _____

6:00 _____

7:00 _____

8:00 _____

9:00 _____

10:00 _____

11:00 _____

12:00 _____

Day 6

7:00	_____
8:00	_____
9:00	_____
10:00	_____
11:00	_____
12:00	_____
1:00	_____
2:00	_____
3:00	_____
4:00	_____
5:00	_____
6:00	_____
7:00	_____
8:00	_____
9:00	_____
10:00	_____
11:00	_____
12:00	_____

Day 7

7:00	_____
8:00	_____
9:00	_____
10:00	_____
11:00	_____
12:00	_____
1:00	_____
2:00	_____
3:00	_____
4:00	_____
5:00	_____
6:00	_____
7:00	_____

8:00   _____

9:00   _____

10:00 _____

11:00 _____

12:00 _____

2. At the end of seven days total the hours you spent doing different activities. Here are some suggested categories. Add more if desired.

Job.   Watching television.
Sleeping.   Yard work.
Eating/meal preparation.   Hobbies.
Grocery shopping.   Commuting.
Other shopping.   Reading.
Playing with children.   Housecleaning.
Playing with significant other.   Laundry.

3. Rewrite your list and rank the categories based on the amount of time you spent on each. Start with the activities that are the most time-consuming.

_____   _____

_____   _____

_____   _____

_____   _____

_____   _____

4. What values do you demonstrate by the way you choose to spend your time?

_____

_____

_____

5. Which of the values named in the previous answer please you and why?

_____

_____

_____

6. In what ways does your use of time conflict with your personal values?

_____

_____

_____

Remember to bring completed work sheet to your next appointment

SECURITY

GOALS OF THE EXERCISE

1. To suggest that ultimately there are no guarantees in life.
2. To remind the client that in spite of all our efforts, we will one day be gone.
3. To challenge the client to keep these things in mind and to find meaning and direction in life.

TYPES OF PROBLEMS THIS EXERCISE MAY BE MOST USEFUL FOR

- Adjustment disorder.
- Anger management.
- Anxiety.
- Chemical dependence/relapse.
- Dependency.
- Depression.
- Family conflict.
- Intimate relationship conflict.
- Obsessive-compulsive behavior.
- Paranoid ideation.
- Sleep disturbance.
- Spiritual confusion.
- Type A behavior.
- Vocational stress.

SUGGESTIONS FOR PROCESSING THIS EXERCISE WITH CLIENT

a. How have you sought security?
b. To what degree have you been successful?
c. Given that nothing is permanent, on what basis do you make everyday decisions (e.g., how you spend money or make a choice between working and spending time with your family)?

SECURITY

In his book *The Wisdom of Insecurity*, Alan Watts asserts that the more one attempts to gain security, the less secure one feels. Does that square with your experience?

1. List eight things you do to feel secure.

    1. _____
    2. _____
    3. _____
    4. _____
    5. _____
    6. _____
    7. _____
    8. _____

2. To what degree is each of your attempts successful?

    1. _____
    2. _____
    3. _____
    4. _____
    5. _____
    6. _____
    7. _____
    8. _____

3. What is the price you pay for each?

    1. _____
    2. _____
    3. _____
    4. _____
    5. _____
    6. _____
    7. _____
    8. _____

4. Is the outcome worth the price you pay?

    1. _____
    2. _____
    3. _____
    4. _____
    5. _____
    6. _____
    7. _____
    8. _____

5. What alternatives are there to continually seeking security?

    _____
    _____
    _____
    _____

Remember to bring completed work sheet to your next appointment

WHERE DOES IT GO?

GOALS OF THE EXERCISE

1. To encourage clients to examine their actions.
2. To suggest that actions manifest personal values.

TYPES OF PROBLEMS THIS EXERCISE MAY BE MOST USEFUL FOR

- Family conflict.
- Spiritual confusion.
- Type A behavior.
- Vocational stress.

SUGGESTIONS FOR PROCESSING THIS EXERCISE WITH CLIENT

a. In what categories did you spend the most money?
b. In what categories did you spend the least money?
c. What surprised you?
d. What do you like about how you spent your money?
e. How do you want to change?
f. What will be difficult about changing?

WHERE DOES IT GO?

How often do you wonder where your paycheck went? You spend a major portion of your waking hours to get it, and yet where it goes can be a real mystery. Finding out where it goes can tell you a lot about yourself and can give you some ideas about where you might want to make some changes.

1. Track the money you spend for at least a month (longer is better). Keep receipts and write down amounts when you don't get a receipt. At the end of that time, divide your expenses into categories and total them. Here are some suggested categories to get you started. Of course, you can combine, divide, delete, or add to these in any way that is useful to you.

Mortgage/rent	Clothing
Groceries	Haircuts
Alcoholic beverages	Toiletries
Gas/electricity	Books
Telephone	Tapes and CDs
Automobiles/public transportation	Gifts
Auto insurance	Hobbies
Life insurance	Charitable contributions
Medical and dental	Pets
Movies and videos	Furniture
Eating out	Education expenses
School lunches	Savings
Travel	

2. Rewrite your list and rank the categories by the amount of money you spent on each. Start with the categories in which you spent the most money.

1. _____   9. _____

2. _____   10. _____

3. _____   11. _____

4. _____   12. _____

5. _____   13. _____

6. _____   14. _____

7. _____   15. _____

8. _____   16. _____

17. _____   22. _____
18. _____   23. _____
19. _____   24. _____
20. _____   25. _____
21. _____

3. What values do you demonstrate in the way you spend money?

_____
_____
_____

4. Which of the values that you have identified do you esteem most?

_____
_____
_____

5. In what way do your spending habits go against your personal values?

_____
_____
_____

6. In *Your Money or Your Life* Joe Dominguez and Vicki Robin define money as being equivalent to "life energy." You receive only so much life energy when you are born—75 years if you are lucky—and you trade a large percentage of that for your paycheck. How do you feel about the way you are spending your life energy?

_____
_____
_____
_____
_____

Remember to bring completed work sheet to your next appointment

TURN IT LOOSE

LETTING GO

GOALS OF THE EXERCISE

1. To imply that the client doesn't have to think about the problem all the time.
2. To hint that letting go is at least a partial decision.
3. To suggest that symbolic action can be helpful.

TYPES OF PROBLEMS THIS EXERCISE MAY BE MOST USEFUL FOR

- Adjustment disorder.
- Anger management.
- Antisocial behavior.
- Anxiety.
- Chemical dependence/relapse.
- Childhood trauma.
- Cognitive deficit.
- Dependency.
- Depression.
- Dissociation.
- Eating disorder.
- Educational deficit.
- Family conflict.
- Female sexual dysfunction.
- Grief/loss unresolved.
- Impulse control disorder.
- Intimate relationship conflict.
- Legal conflict.
- Low self-esteem.
- Male sexual dysfunction.
- Mania or hypomania.
- Medical issue.
- Obsessive-compulsive behavior.

- Paranoid ideation.
- Phobia-panic/agoraphobia.
- Psychoticism.
- Sexual abuse.
- Sleep disturbance.
- Social discomfort.
- Somatization.
- Spiritual confusion.
- Suicidal ideation.
- Type A behavior.
- Vocational stress.

SUGGESTIONS FOR PROCESSING THIS EXERCISE WITH CLIENT

a. Describe the experience of letting go of the balloon.
b. What do you think happened to your balloon?

LETTING GO

1. Make a list of the things related to the problem that you carry around and which you would be better off without.

   _____

   _____

   _____

   _____

   _____

2. List three places where you feel more relaxed and serene.

   1. _____

   2. _____

   3. _____

3. Buy a helium balloon and several ribbons. On each ribbon write one of the things that you would like to let go of and tie it to the balloon.

4. Go to one of the places where you feel relaxed and, when you are ready, release the balloon.

5. Describe the thoughts and emotions you felt as the balloon drifted away.

   _____

   _____

   _____

6. What do you think happened to your ribbons?

   _____

   _____

   _____

If you find this exercise helpful, you can repeat it as many times as you like.

Remember to bring completed work sheet to your next appointment

DEFINING THE LIMITS OF YOUR INFLUENCE

GOALS OF THE EXERCISE

1. To suggest that the client can control some things while others are beyond one's control.
2. To encourage the client to take action on what can be controlled and to stop wasting precious time and energy on the rest.

TYPES OF PROBLEMS THIS EXERCISE MAY BE MOST USEFUL FOR

- Adjustment disorder.
- Anger management.
- Anxiety.
- Chemical dependence/relapse.
- Childhood trauma.
- Dependency.
- Eating disorder.
- Family conflict.
- Grief/loss unresolved.
- Intimate relationship conflict.
- Legal conflict.
- Low self-esteem.
- Medical issue.
- Obsessive-compulsive behavior.
- Paranoid ideation.
- Phobia-panic/agoraphobia.
- Psychoticism.
- Sexual abuse.
- Sleep disturbance.
- Social discomfort.
- Spiritual confusion.
- Suicidal ideation.

- Type A behavior.
- Vocational stress.

SUGGESTIONS FOR PROCESSING THIS EXERCISE WITH CLIENT

a. What can you control in the problem situation?
b. What is beyond your control?
c. What will happen if you stop trying to control the things that are outside of your control?
d. How do you know that it is time to stop trying to control something?

DEFINING THE LIMITS OF YOUR INFLUENCE

In every situation, there are a huge number of factors that one can control and many others that one cannot control. Are you wasting precious time and energy on the things you cannot control?

1. Write five or more things about your problem situation that you can control.
    1. _____
    2. _____
    3. _____
    4. _____
    5. _____

2. How do you control each of these things?
    1. _____
    2. _____
    3. _____
    4. _____
    5. _____

3. Write below five or more things about your problem situation that you cannot control.
    1. _____
    2. _____
    3. _____
    4. _____
    5. _____

4. In what ways have you tried to control these things and what has been your degree of success?

    1. _____
    2. _____
    3. _____
    4. _____
    5. _____

5. At what point will you decide to stop using your energy to control things that are beyond your ability to control, and what will you do instead?

    _____

    _____

    _____

    _____

    _____

Suggestion: Review this page frequently. As you find new things that you can control, add them to that list. As you stop trying to control things, add them to the list of things you cannot control. Consider the things you control and how you gained that power. How can this knowledge be applied to other situations?

Remember to bring completed work sheet to your next appointment

FORGIVENESS

GOALS OF THE EXERCISE

1. To suggest that forgiveness is a decision that carries some benefits.
2. To challenge the client either to get satisfaction from the other person or to let go of the urge to get even.

TYPES OF PROBLEMS THIS EXERCISE MAY BE MOST USEFUL FOR

- Anger management.
- Antisocial behavior.
- Childhood trauma.
- Dependency.
- Depression.
- Family conflict.
- Grief/loss unresolved.
- Impulse control disorder.
- Intimate relationship conflict.
- Paranoid ideation.
- Vocational stress.

SUGGESTIONS FOR PROCESSING THIS EXERCISE WITH CLIENT

a. What do you feel you are owed by the other person?
b. What are the advantages and disadvantages of remaining angry?
c. Have you let the other person know what you want?
d. How will you know that you have forgiven the other person?

FORGIVENESS

While it is common for people to hold a grudge when they have been wronged, there is a growing body of evidence that suggests that unresolved anger is bad for your physical and mental health. It may be impossible and even undesirable to forget what happened, but granting forgiveness can also provide you with many benefits. What is forgiveness? A popular definition holds that when you forgive, you simply write off any debt that you feel is owed to you. In other words, it is a decision.

1. What do you rightfully deserve that would even the score (in "an eye for an eye" sense of justice)?

   _____

   _____

2. What price do you pay for holding onto this debt?

   _____

   _____

3. Have you let the other person know what you think you deserve?

   _____

4. If not, could you?

   _____

5. Can the other person or is he or she willing to give you what you want?

   _____

   _____

6. How would you be better off if you were to give up on getting even?

   _____

   _____

7. For how long are you willing to continue to harbor your anger?

   _____

   _____

Remember to bring completed work sheet to your next appointment

HANGING ON OR HOLDING BACK?

1. To question whether doing something for someone is in that person's best interest.
2. To suggest that others have skills of their own.
3. To propose the idea that the client isn't responsible for everything that happens to everyone.
4. To remind the client that there are consequences for ignoring one's own needs.

TYPES OF PROBLEMS THIS EXERCISE MAY BE MOST USEFUL FOR

- Anxiety.
- Chemical dependence/relapse.
- Childhood trauma.
- Dependency.
- Depression.
- Family conflict.
- Intimate relationship conflict.
- Low self-esteem.
- Spiritual confusion.
- Suicidal ideation.
- Type A behavior.

SUGGESTIONS FOR PROCESSING THIS EXERCISE WITH CLIENT

a. How have you tried to help or protect the other person?
b. Where have you succeeded?
c. Where have you been less successful?
d. What have your efforts cost you?
e. What alternatives do you see? (If the client sees only "either-or" possibilities, suggest a "both-and" solution.)

HANGING ON OR HOLDING BACK?

Watching someone you love engage in dangerous or self-destructive behavior can be painful. Sometimes it is even more painful to try to protect them, and in the long run, your actions can prevent them from learning the consequences of their actions.

1. Name five ways you have tried to protect the other person.

    1. _____
    2. _____
    3. _____
    4. _____
    5. _____

2. Name five or more ways that your attempts to protect accomplished your intentions.

    1. _____
    2. _____
    3. _____
    4. _____
    5. _____

3. Name five or more ways that your attempts have failed.

    1. _____
    2. _____
    3. _____
    4. _____
    5. _____

4. What have been the costs to you in the following areas? Be specific.

   Emotionally

   _____

   _____

   _____

   Physically

   _____

   _____

   _____

   Financially

   _____

   _____

   _____

5. If you hadn't taken the steps you took, where would the other person be now?

   _____

   _____

   _____

6. Where would you be?

   _____

   _____

   _____

7. How long are you willing to continue as you have in the past? Be specific.

   _____

   _____

   _____

8. If you want to do something different, what alternatives do you see? Alternatives include anything other than what you have been doing.

   _____

   _____

   _____

9. What would be the cost or risk of each?

    _____

    _____

    _____

10. What would be the possible rewards?

    _____

    _____

    _____

Remember to bring completed work sheet to your next appointment

THINK!

TIME-OUT!!!

GOALS OF THE EXERCISE

1. To suggest that new behaviors can replace old behaviors.
2. To imply that the client doesn't have to base actions on feelings.
3. To point out that the client can take time in solving problems.
4. To propose the idea that one's thinking is clearer when one is not overly emotional.

TYPES OF PROBLEMS THIS EXERCISE MAY BE MOST USEFUL FOR

- Anger management.
- Family conflict.
- Impulse control disorder.
- Intimate relationship conflict.

SUGGESTIONS FOR PROCESSING THIS EXERCISE WITH CLIENT

a. How did you remember to call time-out?
b. If there were times you forgot, what did you learn from them?
c. What was helpful to think about during the time-out?

TIME-OUT!!!

Every coach worth his or her salt knows that when the momentum goes against you, a time-out will often turn the tide. Likewise, many parents find it helpful to call time-out when the children are getting a bit frisky. A time-out gives you an opportunity to take time to think about what you are trying to accomplish and to get back on track.

1. List the indicators that tell you the problem is starting to get out of control. Note physical changes in yourself and others, thoughts, actions, words, or anything that sets off your alarms.

   _____

   _____

   _____

   _____

   _____

2. Talk to others who may be involved if necessary. Explain that the purpose of time-out is to improve your relationship and to try to enlist their participation in solving the problem. Explain that if one of you calls time-out, you're not refusing to talk about an issue; rather, you are just taking time to reflect so you can then communicate in a thoughtful way. Agree among yourselves what words or actions you will use to initiate a time-out. Write those below:

   _____

   _____

   _____

   _____

   _____

3. Track the time and dates that you call time-out.

   1. Date: _____   Time: _____

      Who called time-out?

      _____

What tipped you off it was time for a break?

_____

_____

_____

What did you think about during the break?

_____

_____

_____

How did the time-out change the interaction?

_____

_____

_____

2. Date: _____   Time: _____

Who called time-out?

_____

What tipped you off it was time for a break?

_____

_____

_____

What did you think about during the break?

_____

_____

_____

How did the time-out change the interaction?

_____

_____

_____

3. Date: _____   Time: _____

Who called time-out?

_____

What tipped you off it was time for a break?

_____

_____

_____

What did you think about during the break?

_____

_____

_____

How did the time-out change the interaction?

_____

_____

_____

Suggestion: Remember that each time you call a time-out you are succeeding in your effort to change the old pattern of interaction. You can call time-out as many times as you feel is necessary. Better to take a break than to do something you might later regret.

Remember to bring completed work sheet to your next appointment

STACKING THE DECK

GOALS OF THE EXERCISE

1. To suggest that the client has resources he or she may not be using.
2. To offer a method that reminds the client of these resources at the time they are needed.

TYPES OF PROBLEMS THIS EXERCISE MAY BE MOST USEFUL FOR

- Anger management.
- Antisocial behavior.
- Chemical dependence/relapse.
- Eating disorder.
- Impulse control disorder.
- Intimate relationship conflict.
- Low self-esteem.

SUGGESTIONS FOR PROCESSING THIS EXERCISE WITH CLIENT

a. Explain each card you have made.
b. Which cards have been the most helpful?
c. How did you use the cards?
d. What did you learn from this exercise?

STACKING THE DECK

Old habits can be hard to break, but often remembering why you want to break them can be enough to make a difference. This exercise is designed to help you remember your reasons "in the heat of battle."

1. Get a stack of 3 × 5 cards and on each one depict a reason you want to change your behavior. You can do this with words, pictures, drawings, or anything that will most powerfully bring the idea to your awareness. Create as many cards and ideas as you can. Be on the lookout for new reasons to change and make new cards as you get new ideas.

2. Keep your cards and this work sheet close at hand. Whenever you have a choice to make between your old behavior and a new one, look at your cards. In the space below, keep track of the dates and times you refer to your cards. Note which reason was most helpful in helping you choose a new behavior. On the day before your next session, answer the questions.

Date   *Time*   *Reason*

_____   _____   _____

_____   _____   _____

_____   _____   _____

_____   _____   _____

_____   _____   _____

3. Which reason or reasons helped you change your behavior most?

_____

4. What does this say about you?

_____

5. What have you learned from this exercise?

_____

6. How can you use what you have learned in the future?

_____

_____

Remember to bring completed work sheet to your next appointment

FAMILY MEETING

GOALS OF THE EXERCISE

1. To encourage the client(s) to take time to formally address issues that may never have been discussed previously.
2. To suggest that everyone involved in the problem can participate in the solution.

TYPES OF PROBLEMS THIS EXERCISE MAY BE MOST USEFUL FOR

- Family conflict.
- Intimate relationship conflict.

SUGGESTIONS FOR PROCESSING THIS EXERCISE WITH CLIENT

a. Review the list of chores and who is doing them.
b. How did you decide who would do what?
c. What improvements have you noticed in how the chores are done?
d. What can you do to keep the ball rolling?
e. Where do you want to make more changes?

FAMILY MEETING

The everyday demands of keeping a home together can create a great opportunity for developing problem-solving and organizational skills. This is an exercise designed to help you rethink the way work gets done around your home.

1. On a separate piece of paper, make a list of all the chores that go into keeping the household operating. Take enough time to make a complete list and be sure to include even the smallest or most mundane tasks. When your list is complete, hold a family meeting. Approach the issue of doing the chores as one that involves everyone in the house. Be sure that each chore is clearly understood (who, what, when, and where). As a group, divide the chores in a way that is fair. Write down who will do each chore and when it will be done.

2. How did you decide who would do what?

   _____

   _____

   _____

3. What other ways did you consider?

   _____

   _____

   _____

4. How will you be sure the chores are completed?

   _____

   _____

   _____

5. When will you talk about this again?

   _____

6. What will you do if someone wants to make changes?

   _____

   _____

   _____

Remember to bring completed work sheet to your next appointment

KEEP ON TRUCKIN'

RECYCLING

GOALS OF THE EXERCISE

1. To imply that the client is resourceful.
2. To point out that the client has been making efforts even if they have been unsuccessful.
3. To encourage the client to look for ideas from his or her own experience.
4. To propose that the client examine his or her approach to problem solving.

TYPES OF PROBLEMS THIS EXERCISE MAY BE MOST USEFUL FOR

- Adjustment disorder.
- Anger management.
- Antisocial behavior.
- Anxiety.
- Chemical dependence/relapse.
- Childhood trauma.
- Cognitive deficit.
- Dependency.
- Depression.
- Dissociation.
- Eating disorder.
- Educational deficit.
- Family conflict.
- Female sexual dysfunction.
- Grief/loss unresolved.
- Impulse control disorder.
- Intimate relationship conflict.
- Legal conflict.
- Low self-esteem.
- Male sexual dysfunction.
- Mania or hypomania.

- Medical issue.
- Obsessive-compulsive behavior.
- Paranoid ideation.
- Phobia-panic/agoraphobia.
- Psychoticism.
- Sexual abuse.
- Sleep disturbance.
- Social discomfort.
- Somatization.
- Spiritual confusion.
- Suicidal ideation.
- Type A behavior.
- Vocational stress.

SUGGESTIONS FOR PROCESSING THIS EXERCISE WITH CLIENT

a. What have you tried?
b. Where did you get that idea?
c. What can you say about how you approach problem solving?
d. What does this suggest that you might want to try in the future?

RECYCLING

At times it can be helpful to review attempts that you have made in the past to solve the problem. Take some time to think about the things you have tried so you can discuss them in your next session.

1. List at least five ways (more is better) that you have tried to deal with your problem. Think about where you got the idea to do it that way. For each, list three things that you have learned about yourself, problem solving, or others.

   Method 1
   Where did you get the idea for method 1?

   _____

   _____

   _____

   What did you like about this method?

   _____

   _____

   _____

   What were its disadvantages?

   _____

   _____

   _____

   Method 2
   Where did you get the idea for method 2?

   _____

   _____

   _____

   What did you like about this method?

   _____

   _____

   _____

What were its disadvantages?

_____

_____

_____

Method 3
Where did you get the idea for method 3?

_____

_____

_____

What did you like about this method?

_____

_____

_____

What were its disadvantages?

_____

_____

_____

Method 4
Where did you get the idea for method 4?

_____

_____

_____

What did you like about this method?

_____

_____

_____

What were its disadvantages?

_____

_____

_____

Method 5
Where did you get the idea for method 5?

_____

_____

_____

What did you like about this method?

_____

_____

_____

What were its disadvantages?

_____

_____

_____

Remember to bring completed work sheet to your next appointment

DEFINE FAILURE/
WHAT KEPT YOU FROM IT?

GOALS OF THE EXERCISE

1. To introduce the idea that there are degrees of success.
2. To imply that the client has some influence over the problem situation.
3. To suggest that the client has skills that may be useful in solving the problem situation.

TYPES OF PROBLEMS THIS EXERCISE MAY BE MOST USEFUL FOR

- Adjustment disorder.
- Anger management.
- Anxiety.
- Chemical dependence/relapse.
- Childhood trauma.
- Dependency.
- Depression.
- Dissociation.
- Eating disorder.
- Family conflict.
- Female sexual dysfunction.
- Grief/loss unresolved.
- Impulse control disorder.
- Intimate relationship conflict.
- Legal conflict.
- Low self-esteem.
- Male sexual dysfunction.
- Mania or hypomania.
- Medical issue.
- Obsessive-compulsive behavior.
- Paranoid ideation.
- Phobia-panic/agoraphobia.

- Psychoticism.
- Sexual abuse.
- Sleep disturbance.
- Social discomfort.
- Somatization.
- Spiritual confusion.
- Suicidal ideation.
- Type A behavior.
- Vocational stress.

SUGGESTIONS FOR PROCESSING THIS EXERCISE WITH CLIENT

a. What did you do to prevent total failure?
b. How can you use that information?

DEFINE FAILURE/
WHAT KEPT YOU FROM IT?

When faced with a problem we often feel that we have failed if we don't find a total solution to it. Another way to think about it is that if the absolute worst doesn't happen, you have had some measure of success. Anything you do that prevents total failure can give you clues about what you might do to deal effectively with the problem.

1. What is your definition of *total* failure in dealing with your problem? In other words, what would have to be true for it to be absolutely impossible for things to get worse?

   _____

   _____

   _____

2. Each time you find yourself in the problem situation, answer two questions: What did you do that prevented total failure? What could you have done that would have guaranteed total failure?

3. Date: _____ Time: _____

   Briefly describe incident:

   _____

   _____

   _____

   What did you do that prevented total failure?

   _____

   _____

   _____

   What could you have done that would have guaranteed total failure?

   _____

   _____

   _____

4. Date: _____ Time: _____

   Briefly describe incident:

   _____

   _____

   _____

   What did you do that prevented total failure?

   _____

   _____

   _____

   What could you have done that would have guaranteed total failure?

   _____

   _____

   _____

5. Date: _____ Time: _____

   Briefly describe incident:

   _____

   _____

   _____

   What did you do that prevented total failure?

   _____

   _____

   _____

   What could you have done that would have guaranteed total failure?

   _____

   _____

   _____

Remember to bring completed work sheet to your next appointment

WHAT NEXT?

GOALS OF THE EXERCISE

1. To suggest that the client can respond to difficult situations.
2. To build rapport by joining the client's efforts.

TYPES OF PROBLEMS THIS EXERCISE MAY BE MOST USEFUL FOR

- Anxiety.
- Obsessive-compulsive behavior.

SUGGESTIONS FOR PROCESSING THIS EXERCISE WITH CLIENT

a. What did you worry about?
b. What happened when you did this exercise?

WHAT NEXT?

It's easy to forget that we have resources, especially when we are faced with difficult situations. This exercise challenges you to catch yourself in the act of worrying and helps you to remember that even if something bad happens, you have a choice in how you respond to it.

1. Keep this paper and a pen or pencil with you at all times.

2. Each time you find yourself worrying about what will happen, record your concern on this page.

3. Assuming that those things will happen, write at least three (or more) things you might do then.

4. What could happen:

   _____

   Possible ways I could respond:
   1. _____
   2. _____
   3. _____

   How would this affect your ability to do the work that gives your life meaning?

   _____

   _____

   _____

5. What could happen:

   _____

   Possible ways I could respond:
   1. _____
   2. _____
   3. _____

   How would this affect your ability to do the work that gives your life meaning?

   _____

   _____

   _____

6. What could happen:

_____

Possible ways I could respond:

1. _____
2. _____
3. _____

How would this affect your ability to do the work that gives your life meaning?

_____

_____

_____

Suggestion: Remember that bad things happen in everyone's lives. What's more important than what happens to you is what you do about it.

Remember to bring completed work sheet to your next appointment

Section XVII

PUT YOUR EXPERIENCE TO WORK

FINDING VALUE IN YOUR EXPERIENCE

GOALS OF THE EXERCISE

1. To remind the client that pain is a necessary part of life.
2. To suggest that painful experiences can be learning experiences.
3. To point out that skills can be generalized.
4. To help the client see the current situation from the perspective of one's entire life.

TYPES OF PROBLEMS THIS EXERCISE MAY BE MOST USEFUL FOR

- Adjustment disorder.
- Anger management.
- Antisocial behavior.
- Anxiety.
- Chemical dependence/relapse.
- Childhood trauma.
- Cognitive deficit.
- Dependency.
- Depression.
- Dissociation.
- Eating disorder.
- Educational deficit.
- Family conflict.
- Female sexual dysfunction.
- Grief/loss unresolved.
- Impulse control disorder.
- Intimate relationship conflict.
- Legal conflict.
- Low self-esteem.
- Male sexual dysfunction.
- Mania or hypomania.

- Medical issue.
- Obsessive-compulsive behavior.
- Paranoid ideation.
- Phobia-panic/agoraphobia.
- Psychoticism.
- Sexual abuse.
- Sleep disturbance.
- Social discomfort.
- Somatization.
- Spiritual confusion.
- Suicidal ideation.
- Type A behavior.
- Vocational stress.

SUGGESTIONS FOR PROCESSING THIS EXERCISE WITH CLIENT

a. What have you learned from your experience?
b. Where else can this learning be helpful?
c. What does this say about you?

FINDING VALUE IN YOUR EXPERIENCE

In spite of what the popular media tell us, it is impossible to live a pain-free life. Even many of life's most important lessons are accompanied by pain. When pain is unavoidable, it is often helpful to find meaning in the experience.

1. What have you learned from your experience of this problem?

   _____

   _____

   _____

2. Name three or more skills you have used in dealing with this problem.

   1. _____

   2. _____

   3. _____

3. In what other parts of your life can you use these skills?

   _____

   _____

   _____

4. Describe how this experience has changed or will change the way you deal with others. Think of specific people and specific things that will change.

   _____

   _____

   _____

5. How does solving this problem help you accomplish the work that gives your life meaning?

   _____

   _____

   _____

6. How does this experience change the way you think about yourself?

   _____

   _____

   _____

Remember to bring completed work sheet to your next appointment

WRITE A LETTER TO YOURSELF

GOALS OF THE EXERCISE

1. To help the client apply what is learned from this situation to other situations.
2. To point out that the client is learning.
3. To provide a resource to be used when later difficulties arise.

TYPES OF PROBLEMS THIS EXERCISE MAY BE MOST USEFUL FOR

- Adjustment disorder.
- Anger management.
- Anxiety.
- Chemical dependence/relapse.
- Childhood trauma.
- Cognitive deficit.
- Dependency.
- Depression.
- Dissociation.
- Eating disorder.
- Educational deficit.
- Family conflict.
- Female sexual dysfunction.
- Grief/loss unresolved.
- Impulse control disorder.
- Intimate relationship conflict.
- Legal conflict.
- Low self-esteem.
- Male sexual dysfunction.
- Mania or hypomania.
- Medical issue.
- Obsessive-compulsive behavior.

- Paranoid ideation.
- Phobia-panic/agoraphobia.
- Psychoticism.
- Sexual abuse.
- Sleep disturbance.
- Social discomfort.
- Somatization.
- Spiritual confusion.
- Suicidal ideation.
- Type A behavior.
- Vocational stress.

SUGGESTIONS FOR PROCESSING THIS EXERCISE WITH CLIENT

a. What have you learned that will be important for you to remember?
b. How will you know that it is time to review your letter?

WRITE A LETTER TO YOURSELF

Now that you have made progress toward your goals, it might be helpful to find a way to make sure you don't forget what you have learned.

1. Write a letter to yourself. The purpose of this letter is to help you should you ever find yourself in a situation similar to the one that brought you to counseling. Tell yourself anything that you think might be useful. Include the things that you or others have done that have been helpful to you.
   Some possibilities include:

   > Acknowledgement of feelings.
   > Appreciation of efforts.
   > Encouragement.
   > Reminder that feelings are temporary.
   > Actions you have taken that helped.
   > Reminder of skills and abilities you have.
   > Places to find support.
   > People, places, and things to avoid.

2. When you have finished, put this letter in a place where you can find it if you start to slip back into your old habits.

   If you like, you may bring your letter to your next appointment for discussion

Section XVIII

RELAPSE PREVENTION

ANTIDOTES

GOALS OF THE EXERCISE

1. To suggest that the client has resources that he or she may not be using.
2. To indicate that a solution used in the past may work again.

TYPES OF PROBLEMS THIS EXERCISE MAY BE MOST USEFUL FOR

- Adjustment disorder.
- Anger management.
- Antisocial behavior.
- Anxiety.
- Chemical dependence/relapse.
- Childhood trauma.
- Cognitive deficit.
- Dependency.
- Depression.
- Dissociation.
- Eating disorder.
- Educational deficit.
- Family conflict.
- Female sexual dysfunction.
- Grief/loss unresolved.
- Impulse control disorder.
- Intimate relationship conflict.
- Legal conflict.
- Low self-esteem.
- Male sexual dysfunction.
- Mania or hypomania.
- Medical issue.
- Obsessive-compulsive behavior.
- Paranoid ideation.

- Phobia-panic/agoraphobia.
- Psychoticism.
- Sexual abuse.
- Sleep disturbance.
- Social discomfort.
- Somatization.
- Spiritual confusion.
- Suicidal ideation.
- Type A behavior.
- Vocational stress.

SUGGESTIONS FOR PROCESSING THIS EXERCISE WITH CLIENT

a. Where did you get your ideas?
b. How will you realize that it is time to refer to this page?

ANTIDOTES

It can be especially hard to think when you are in the middle of a crisis. This exercise helps you get your ideas together so they will be available when you need them.

1. Make a list of 10 or more things that you can do when your problem starts to cause you trouble. These may be things that have worked in the past, things that others have recommended, or things that you think might work but haven't yet tried. They can include people you can call on for help, things you might say to yourself, prayers, actions you can take or not take, or anything else you think might work.

   1. _____
   2. _____
   3. _____
   4. _____
   5. _____
   6. _____
   7. _____
   8. _____
   9. _____
   10. _____

Suggestion: As you get new ideas, add them to the list. Mark the ideas that are particularly helpful. Keep this list in a place where you can find it quickly, and refer to it when you need some ideas on how to deal with the problem.

Remember to bring completed work sheet to your next appointment

ARMING THE ALARM SYSTEM

GOALS OF THE EXERCISE

1. To suggest that the client has learned important information that may be helpful in the future.
2. To remind the client that past solutions can be helpful in the present and in the future.

TYPES OF PROBLEMS THIS EXERCISE MAY BE MOST USEFUL FOR

- Adjustment disorder.
- Anger management.
- Antisocial behavior.
- Anxiety.
- Chemical dependence/relapse.
- Childhood trauma.
- Cognitive deficit.
- Dependency.
- Depression.
- Dissociation.
- Eating disorder.
- Educational deficit.
- Family conflict.
- Female sexual dysfunction.
- Grief/loss unresolved.
- Impulse control disorder.
- Intimate relationship conflict.
- Legal conflict.
- Low self-esteem.
- Male sexual dysfunction.
- Mania or hypomania.
- Medical issue.

- Obsessive-compulsive behavior.
- Paranoid ideation.
- Phobia-panic/agoraphobia.
- Psychoticism.
- Sexual abuse.
- Sleep disturbance.
- Social discomfort.
- Somatization.
- Spiritual confusion.
- Suicidal ideation.
- Type A behavior.
- Vocational stress.

SUGGESTIONS FOR PROCESSING THIS EXERCISE WITH CLIENT

a. What will warn you that you may be falling into an old pattern?
b. How will you respond?
c. What is the most important thing for you to remember from this experience?

ARMING THE ALARM SYSTEM

Now that you have had some success in dealing with your problem, it may be helpful to clarify what you have learned so that you can have ideas for future reference if necessary.

1. List five (or more) things that will warn you that you are starting to slip back into your old ways and the problem is threatening to gain the upper hand. Focus on the earliest and smallest warning signs. For each, make a plan of how you will respond.

   1. Warning sign:

   _____

   How I could respond:

   _____

   _____

   _____

   2. Warning sign:

   _____

   How I could respond:

   _____

   _____

   _____

   3. Warning sign:

   _____

   How I could respond:

   _____

   _____

   _____

   4. Warning sign:

   _____

How I could respond:

_____

_____

_____

5. Warning sign:

_____

How I could respond:

_____

_____

_____

Suggestion: Put this page in a place where you will remember it. If you notice any warning signs that you have identified, or if something else comes up that arouses your alarm, refer to this paper for ideas on how to respond.

Remember to bring completed work sheet to your next appointment

BIBLIOGRAPHY

deShazer, Steve. 1985. *Keys to Solution in Brief Therapy*. New York: Norton.

Dominguez, Joseph R., and Vicki Robin. 1992. *Your Money or Your Life: Transforming Your Relationship with Money and Achieving Financial Independence*. New York: Viking.

Haley, Jay. 1986. *The Power Tactics of Jesus Christ and Other Essays*. Second Edition. New York: Triangle Press, Distributed by Norton.

Hudson, Patricia O., and William H. O'Hanlon. 1992. *Rewriting Love Stories: Brief Marital Therapy*. New York: Norton.

Jones, Morgan D. 1995. *The Thinker's Toolkit: Fourteen Skills for Making Smarter Decisions in Business and in Life*. New York: Random House.

Keeney, Bradford P. 1990. *Improvisational Therapy: A Practical Guide for Creative Clinical Strategies*. New York: Guilford Press.

Michalko, Michael. 1991. *Thinkertoys: A Handbook of Business Creativity for the 90s*. Berkeley, CA: Ten Speed Press.

O'Hanlon, William H. 1987. *Taproots: Underlying Principles of Milton Erickson's Therapy and Hypnosis*. New York: Norton.

O'Hanlon, William H., and A. L. Hexum. 1990. *An Uncommon Casebook: The Complete Clinical Work of Milton H. Erickson, M.D.* New York: Norton.

O'Hanlon, William H., and Michele Weiner-Davis. 1989. *In Search of Solutions: A New Direction in Psychotherapy*. New York: Norton.

von Oech, Roger. 1993. *A Whack on the Side of the Head: How You Can Be More Creative*. Revised Edition. New York: Warner Books.

Watts, Alan W. 1951. *The Wisdom of Insecurity*. New York: Vintage Books.

Watzlawick, Paul, John H. Weakland, and R. Fisch. 1974. *Change: Principles of Problem Formation and Problem Resolution*. New York: Norton.

QUICK CROSS-REFERENCE
PROBLEM/ASSIGNMENT GUIDE

Adjustment Disorder
Exercises I.A, I.B, II.A, III.A, III.B, III.C, IV.A, IV.C, IV.D, V.B, V.C, V.D, VI.A, VI.B, VII.A, VII.B, VII.C, VIII.B, VIII.C, IX.D, IX.E, X.A, X.D, XI.C, XII.C, XIII.C, XIV.A, XIV.B, XVI.A, XVI.B, XVII.A, XVII.B, XVIII.A, XVIII.B

Anger Management
Exercises I.A, I.B, II.A, II.B, II.C, III.A, III.B, III.C, III.D, IV.A, IV.B, IV.C, IV.E, V.B, V.C, VI.A, VI.C, VI.D, VII.A, VII.B, VII.C, VIII.B, VIII.C, IX.B, IX.C, IX.D, IX.E, X.B, X.D, XII.A, XIII.C, XIV.A, XIV.B, XIV.C, XV.A, XV.B, XVI.A, XVI.B, XVII.A, XVII.B, XVIII.A, XVIII.B

Antisocial Behavior
Exercises I.B, II.A, III.A, III.B, III.D, IV.A, IV.C, V.B, V.C, VI.C, VI.D, VII.A, VII.C, VIII.C, IX.C, IX.D, IX.E, XIV.A, XIV.C, XV.B, XVI.A, XVII.A, XVIII.A, XVIII.B

Anxiety
Exercises I.A, I.B, II.A, II.B, III.A, III.B, III.C, IV.A, IV.B, IV.C, IV.D, IV.E, V.A, V.B, V.C, VI.A, VI.B, VI.C, VII.A, VII.B, VIII.A, VIII.B, VIII.C, IX.D, IX.E, X.A, X.B, X.D, XI.C, XII.B, XII.C, XIII.A, XIII.C, XIV.A, XIV.B, XIV.D, XVI.A, XVI.B, XVI.C, XVII.A, XVII.B, XVIII.A, XVIII.B

Chemical Dependence/Relapse
Exercises I.A, I.B, II.A, II.B, III.A, III.B, III.C, IV.A, IV.B, IV.C, IV.D, V.B, V.C, VI.A, VI.B, VII.A, VII.C, VIII.B, VIII.C, IX.B, IX.C, IX.D, IX.E, X.A, XIII.C, XIV.A, XIV.B, XIV.D, XV.B, XVI.A, XVI.B, XVII.A, XVII.B, XVIII.A, XVIII.B

Childhood Trauma
Exercises I.A, II.A, III.A, III.B, III.C, IV.A, IV.B, IV.C, V.B, V.C, VI.A, VI.B, VII.A, VII.B, VII.C, VIII.B, VIII.C, IX.D, IX.E, X.A, XIV.A, XIV.B, XIV.C, XIV.D, XVI.A, XVI.B, XVII.A, XVII.B, XVIII.A, XVIII.B

Cognitive Deficit
Exercises III.C, IV.C, V.B, VII.A, VII.C, VIII.C, IX.D, IX.E, X.A, XIV.A, XVI.A, XVII.A, XVIII.A, XVIII.B

Dependency
Exercises I.A, I.B, II.A, II.B, III.A, III.B, III.C, III.D, IV.A, IV.C, IV.D, IV.E, V.B, V.C, VI.A, VI.B, VI.C, VI.D, VII.A, VII.B, VII.C, VIII.B, VIII.C, IX.B, IX.C, IX.D, IX.E, X.A, X.D, XI.C, XII.A, XII.B, XII.C, XII.D, XIII.C, XIV.A, XIV.B, XIV.C, XIV.D, XVI.A, XVI.B, XVII.A, XVII.B, XVIII.A, XVIII.B

Depression
Exercises I.A, I.B, II.A, II.B, III.A, III.B, III.C, III.D, IV.A, IV.B, IV.C, IV.D, IV.E, V.A, V.B, V.C, VI.A, VI.B, VI.C, VI.D, VII.A, VII.B, VIII.A, VIII.B, VIII.C, IX.A, IX.C, IX.D, IX.E, X.A, X.D, XII.A, XII.B, XII.C, XII.D, XIII.A, XIII.C, XIV.A, XIV.C, XIV.D, XVI.A, XVI.B, XVII.A, XVII.B, XVIII.A, XVIII.B

Dissociation
Exercises I.A, II.A, III.A

Eating Disorder
Exercises I.A, I.B, II.A, III.A, III.B, III.C, IV.A, IV.B, IV.C, V.B, V.C, VI.A, VII.A, VII.B, VII.C, VIII.B, VIII.C, IX.B, IX.D, IX.E, XIV.A, XIV.B, XV.B, XVI.A, XVI.B, XVII.A, XVII.B, XVIII.A, XVIII.B

Educational Deficit
Exercises I.B, II.A, III.C, IV.C, V.B, V.C, VII.A, VII.C, VIII.C, IX.D, IX.E, X.A, XIV.A, XVI.A, XVII.A, XVII.B, XVIII.A, XVIII.B

Family Conflict
Exercises I.A, I.B, II.A, II.B, II.C, III.A, III.B, III.C, III.D, IV.A, IV.B, IV.C, IV.D, IV.E, V.B, V.C, VI.A, VI.B, VI.C, VI.D, VII.A, VII.C, VIII.B, VIII.C, IX.B, IX.C, IX.D, IX.E, X.A, X.B, X.C, XI.C, XII.A, XII.B, XII.D, XIII.B, XIII.C, XIII.D, XIV.A, XIV.B, XIV.C, XIV.D, XV.A, XV.C, XVI.A, XVI.B, XVII.A, XVII.B, XVIII.A, XVIII.B

Female Sexual Dysfunction
Exercises I.A, II.A, III.A, III.B, IV.A, IV.C, V.B, V.C, VII.A, VII.C, VIII.B, VIII.C, IX.C, IX.E, XIV.A, XVI.A, XVI.B, XVII.A, XVII.B, XVIII.A, XVIII.B

Grief/Loss Unresolved
Exercises I.A, II.A, III.A, III.B, III.C, IV.C, V.B, V.C, V.D, VI.B, VII.A, VII.B, VII.C, VIII.B, VIII.C, IX.B, IX.D, IX.E, XIV.A, XIV.B, XIV.C, XVI.A, XVI.B, XVII.A, XVII.B, XVIII.A, XVIII.B

Impulse Control Disorder
Exercises I.A, I.B, II.A, III.A, III.B, IV.A, IV.B, IV.C, V.B, V.C, VI.A, VI.B, VI.C, VII.A, VII.C, VIII.B, VIII.C, IX.B, IX.D, IX.E, XIV.A, XIV.C, XV.A, XV.B, XVI.A, XVI.B, XVII.A, XVII.B, XVIII.A, XVIII.B

Intimate Relationship Conflict
Exercises I.A, I.B, II.A, II.B, III.A, III.B, III.C, III.D, IV.A, IV.C, IV.D, IV.E, V.B, V.C, VI.A, VI.B, VI.C, VI.D, VII.A, VII.B, VII.C, VIII.B, VIII.C, IX.B, IX.C, IX.D, IX.E, X.A, X.C, XI.A, XI.B, XI.C, XII.A, XII.B, XII.C, XII.D, XIII.B, XIII.C, XIV.A, XIV.B, XIV.C, XIV.D, XV.A, XV.B, XV.C, XVI.A, XVI.B, XVII.A, XVII.B, XVIII.A, XVIII.B

Legal Conflict

Exercises II.A, III.A, IV.A, IV.C, IV.E, V.B, VI.B, VI.D, VII.A, VII.C, VIII.C, IX.E, XI.C, XIV.A, XIV.B, XVI.A, XVI.B, XVII.A, XVII.B, XVIII.A, XVIII.B

Low Self-Esteem

Exercises I.A, I.B, II.A, II.B, III.A, III.B, III.C, III.D, IV.A, IV.B, IV.C, IV.D, V.B, V.C, VI.A, VI.B, VI.C, VI.D, VII.A, VII.B, VII.C, VIII.B, VIII.C, IX.A, IX.B, IX.C, IX.D, IX.E, X.A, X.D, XI.A, XII.A, XII.B, XII.C, XII.D, XIV.A, XIV.B, XIV.D, XV.B, XVI.A, XVI.B, XVII.A, XVII.B, XVIII.A, XVIII.B

Male Sexual Dysfunction

Exercises I.A, II.A, III.A, IV.A, IV.C, V.B, V.C, VII.A, VII.C, VIII.B, VIII.C, IX.C, IX.E, XIV.A, XVI.A, XVI.B, XVII.A, XVII.B, XVIII.A, XVIII.B

Mania or Hypomania

Exercises I.A, II.A, III.A, III.B, IV.A, IV.C, V.B, V.C, VII.A, VII.C, VIII.B, VIII.C, IX.D, IX.E, XIV.A, XVI.A, XVI.B, XVII.A, XVII.B, XVIII.A, XVIII.B

Medical Issue

Exercises III.A, III.C, V.B, V.C, VII.A, VII.C, VIII.C, IX.D, IX.E, XIV.A, XIV.B, XVI.A, XVI.B, XVII.A, XVII.B, XVIII.A, XVIII.B

Obsessive-Compulsive Behavior

Exercises I.A, I.B, II.A, II.B, III.A, III.B, III.C, IV.A, IV.B, IV.C, IV.D, IV.E, V.A, V.B, V.C, VI.B, VI.C, VII.A, VII.B, VIII.A, VIII.B, VIII.C, IX.B, IX.D, IX.E, X.A, X.D, XIII.C, XIV.A, XIV.B, XVI.A, XVI.B, XVI.C, XVII.A, XVII.B, XVIII.A, XVIII.B

Paranoid Ideation

Exercises I.A, II.A, III.A, IV.A, IV.B, IV.C, V.B, V.C, VI.C, VII.A, VII.B, VII.C, VIII.B, VIII.C, IX.B, IX.D, IX.E, X.D, XIII.C, XIV.A, XIV.B, XIV.C, XVI.A, XVI.B, XVII.A, XVII.B, XVIII.A, XVIII.B

Phobia-Panic/Agoraphobia

Exercises I.A, I.B, II.A, II.B, III.A, III.B, III.C, IV.A, IV.B, IV.C, V.A, V.B, V.C, VI.A, VI.B, VII.A, VII.B, VII.C, VIII.A, VIII.B, VIII.C, IX.A, IX.B, IX.D, IX.E, X.A, XIV.A, XIV.B, XVI.A, XVI.B, XVII.A, XVII.B, XVIII.A, XVIII.B

Psychoticism

Exercises I.A, II.A, III.A, III.C, IV.A, IV.C, V.B, VII.A, VII.C, VIII.C, IX.D, IX.E, XIV.A, XIV.B, XVI.A, XVI.B, XVII.A, XVII.B, XVIII.A, XVIII.B

Sexual Abuse

Exercises I.A, II.A, III.A, III.B, III.C, IV.C, V.B, V.C, V.D, VII.A, VII.C, VIII.C, IX.B, IX.C, IX.D, IX.E, XIV.A, XIV.B, XVI.A, XVI.B, XVII.A, XVII.B, XVIII.A, XVIII.B

Sleep Disturbance

Exercises I.A, II.A, III.A, III.C, IV.A, IV.C, IV.E, V.A, V.B, V.C, VI.B, VII.A, VIII.A, VIII.B, VIII.C, IX.E, X.A, XIII.C, XIV.A, XIV.B, XVI.A, XVI.B, XVII.A, XVII.B, XVIII.A, XVIII.B

Social Discomfort

Exercises I.A, II.A, II.B, III.A, III.B, III.C, IV.A, IV.B, IV.C, V.B, V.C, VI.A, VI.B, VI.C, VII.A, VII.B, VII.C, VIII.A, VIII.B, VIII.C, IX.D, IX.E, X.A, X.D, XIV.A, XIV.B, XVI.A, XVI.B, XVII.A, XVII.B, XVIII.A, XVIII.B

Somatization

Exercises I.A, II.A, III.A, III.B, IV.A, IV.C, V.B, V.C, VII.A, VII.C, VIII.C, IX.D, IX.E, XIV.A, XVI.A, XVI.B, XVII.A, XVII.B, XVIII.A, XVIII.B

Spiritual Confusion

Exercises I.A, I.B, II.A, III.A, III.B, III.C, IV.A, IV.C, V.B, V.C, VII.A, VII.C, VIII.C, IX.D, IX.E, XI.A, XI.B, XIII.A, XIII.B, XIII.C, XIII.D, XIV.A, XIV.B, XIV.D, XVI.A, XVI.B, XVII.A, XVII.B, XVIII.A, XVIII.B

Suicidal Ideation

Exercises I.A, II.A, III.A, III.B, III.C, IV.A, IV.B, IV.C, V.B, V.C, VI.B, VI.D, VII.A, VII.B, VII.C, VIII.B, VIII.C, IX.D, IX.E, X.A, X.D, XII.C, XIV.A, XIV.B, XIV.D, XVI.A, XVI.B, XVII.A, XVII.B, XVIII.A, XVIII.B

Type A Behavior

Exercises I.A, II.A, II.B, III.A, III.B, III.C, IV.A, IV.B, IV.C, IV.E, V.B, V.C, VI.A, VI.B, VII.A, VII.B, VII.C, VIII.B, VIII.C, IX.A, IX.B, IX.D, IX.E, X.A, XIII.C, XIII.D, XIV.A, XIV.B, XIV.D, XVI.A, XVI.B, XVII.A, XVII.B, XVIII.A, XVIII.B

Vocational Stress

Exercises I.A, II.A, II.C, III.A, III.B, III.C, IV.A, IV.B, IV.C, IV.E, V.B, V.C, VI.A, VI.B, VI.C, VII.A, VII.C, VIII.B, VIII.C, IX.D, IX.E, X.A, XI.B, XI.C, XII.A, XII.C, XIII.B, XIII.C, XIII.D, XIV.A, XIV.B, XIV.C, XVI.A, XVI.B, XVII.A, XVII.B, XVIII.A, XVIII.B

ABOUT THE DISK

INTRODUCTION

The disk contains electronic versions of the exercises printed in this book. The exercises are saved in Microsoft Word for Windows version 6.0. In order to use the files, you need to have word processing software capable of reading Microsoft Word for Windows 6.0 files.

SYSTEM REQUIREMENTS

- IBM PC or compatible computer
- 3.5" floppy disk drive
- Windows 3.1 or higher
- Microsoft Word for Windows version 6.0 or later or other word processing software capable of reading Microsoft Word for Windows 6.0 files.

NOTE: Many popular word processing programs are capable of reading Microsoft Word for Windows 6.0 files. However, users should be aware that a slight amount of formatting might be lost when using a program other than Microsoft Word. If your word processor cannot read Microsoft Word 6.0 files, unformatted text files have been provided in the TXT directory on the floppy disk.

HOW TO INSTALL THE FILES ONTO YOUR COMPUTER

Running the installation program will copy the files to your hard drive in the default directory C:\HOMEWORK. To run the installation program, do the following:

1. Insert the enclosed disk into the floppy disk drive of your computer.

2. Windows 3.1 or NT 3.51: From the Program Manager, choose File, Run.
   Windows 95 or NT 4.0: From the Start Menu, choose Run.

3. Type A:\SETUP and press Enter. The opening screen of the installation program will appear. Press Enter to continue.

4. The default destination directory is C:\HOMEWORK. If you wish to change the default destination, you may do so now. Follow the instructions on the screen.

5. The installation program will copy all files to your hard drive in the C:\HOMEWORK or user-designated directory.

USING THE FILES

Loading Files

To use the word processing files, launch your word processing program (e.g., Microsoft Word or WordPerfect). Select File, Open from the pull-down menu. Select the appropriate drive and directory. If you installed the files to the default directory, the files will be located in the C:\HOMEWORK directory. A list of files should appear. If you do not see a list of files in the directory, you need to select WORD DOCUMENT (*.DOC) under Files of Type. Double click on the file you want to open. Edit the file according to your needs.

Printing Files

If you want to print a file, select File, Print from the pull-down menu.

Saving Files

When you have finished editing a file, you should save it under a new file name before exiting your program.

User Assistance

If you need basic assistance with installation or if you have a damaged disk, please contact Wiley Technical Support at:

Phone: (212) 850-6753
Fax: (212) 850-6800 (Attention: Wiley Technical Support)
Email: techhelp@wiley.com

To place additional orders or to request information about other Wiley products, please call (800) 225-5945.

WILEY